150 Years of Marriage

Ron and Crystal Meinstein

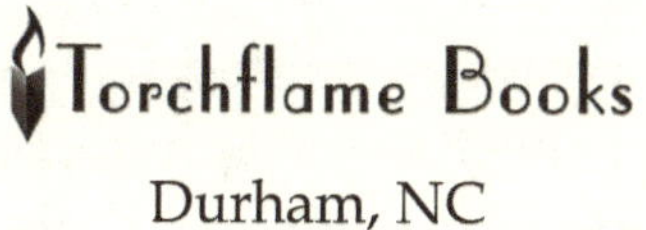

Durham, NC

150 Years of Marriage
Ron and Crystal Meinstein
rmeinstein@live.com

Published 2021, by Torchflame Books
an Imprint of Light Messages
www.lightmessages.com
Durham, NC 27713 USA
SAN: 920-9298

Paperback ISBN: 978-1-61153-387-3
E-book ISBN: 978-1-61153-388-0
Library of Congress Control Number: 2020922977

We dedicate this book to a loving God who brought us together and to the memory of our mothers Maria (Mimi) Meinstein and Mary Jane Carlson and our fathers, Siegfried Meinstein, and James Carlson.

Prologue

My dad always called my mom "Mimi" or "Toots" (short for tootsie), but her real name was Maria. As their son and only child, I grew up somewhat sheltered, even from their past. I knew that mom's family was very poor, and that she grew up in the small lower Bavarian town of Pfarrkirchen, Germany; however, I didn't hear the following story from my mother's childhood until I was in my fifties.

Maria's teacher had asked her to stay after class—not as punishment, but reward. Teachers always loved Maria. She was smart and worked hard. As her teacher graded papers, Maria cleaned and prepped the classroom for the next day while they chatted. It was rare for an eight-year-old to talk freely with her teacher, especially in the strict German schools in the early 1930s. Maria had so little time for friends, with her homework and household chores. She needed to know that someone cared.

As she started home, she remembered it was her day to pick up the milk. Oh no, now she would be really late! She tied her shoes together and started to run. It was a cold November day, but she had to save her shoes for the snow. Besides, she was used to running barefoot. Shoes were hard to come by in her family. Most of her clothes were hand-me-downs from neighbors and friends.

She walked into the dairy barn and politely asked for her family's milk. The heavy bucket sloshed as she strained to hurry off without spilling it. The trip home was almost a mile. About halfway home, her arms and shoulders began to ache. She wanted to stop, but didn't dare. At the bottom of the last hill, she found her father waiting for her.

A third of the milk was gone.

She steeled herself for what she knew was coming. The beatings and profanity weren't what hurt the most; it was the condemnation of her uselessness.

Her mother would try to intervene only for his wrath to turn on her. In addition to the abuse, German politics were turning in the early thirties. A desperate people were hungry for change. That change was on the near horizon marching in goose step.

I wasn't aware of my mother's dark demons. All I knew was that she was always the kindest, most loving mother. Our house was always immaculate, and she was a wonderful, skilled cook. She treated my friends and I like royalty. She would do anything I needed. She was always my soft place to fall.

However, Mom's scars included bouts of paranoia and hallucinations. She would talk about the neighbors sneaking into the house, and stealing or moving clothes and other objects, or sticking me with needles in order to somehow, covertly control my actions. Occasionally, she would come to my school and look in the window to make sure I was still there. It made me uneasy, even scared at times, but it was mom. Despite her periodic eccentricities, no-one has ever loved me more. I did my best to redirect her, or explain what was real and why. Even when she was hospitalized for a short time, I tried to teach her how to say the right things to act normal for the psychiatrist. She usually listened to me. Also, I could usually make her laugh. Somehow, that always seemed to help. Then she would go back to her routine as loving housewife and mother.

It's been said that life is like a tapestry. Each life represents but a single thread. Ultimately, it only makes sense from God's vantage point; only He sees the entire picture. However, through this work, Crystal and I have been blessed to see at least a small part of the picture surrounding us. And now you can too.

I

Ron and Crystal

The cliché, "happily ever after," isn't real life. Life is determined by the moments of time, how we spend them, how we perceive them. If you believe you are happy, life is good. If not, life is bad. Your marital status doesn't determine your happiness. Happiness, for the most part, is a choice. While death is not a choice, a commitment that lasts until death is.

When I met Crystal some forty plus years ago, we began an adventure that is still evolving. When we married, we not only joined our skills and abilities against the many trials to ensue, we also united our families. While families diverge in many forms today, it was obvious that our families were of the increasingly uncommon traditional variety. We all married for better or worse, and although we all saw both over the course of time, we would insist, by far, the good prevailed.

It wasn't long after I met Crystal that, we started talking about our families and our parents' stories. Our parents met during World War II, and we were their baby boomer children. None of our stories was love at first sight. My dad yelled orders at my mom when they met. Crystal's parents met at a USO club (United Service Organizations), and didn't see each other again for more than a year. Crystal didn't trust me when we met. In fact, she thought I was a liar and bit of a cad.

What is truly amazing, and worthy of preservation, are the special moments of each of our three stories. These were the moments that made us who we are, connected us as couples, and put us in an increasingly less familiar rank, of the happily married.

Now it's time for us to share these moments.

Endings and Beginnings

The whole room sat enthralled as Dad reminisced about World War II. As a counterintelligence agent, he had rounded up fugitive war criminals after VE day, including high-level SS officers. He talked animatedly about how he met Mom, a 21-year-old German farm girl, while she was violating the strict military curfew.

All of this was fascinating, but I had heard the stories a hundred times. My mind was racing with all the details we had to address between that evening and Friday. Only a few days to pack up the house, run errands, and completely organize the move. Friday was moving day.

Mom had passed away at age 87, about six months earlier, and we were determined to move Dad closer. My wife, our three daughters, and I could help him more in Columbus, Ohio. He was lonely in his home of fifty-three years in Oak Lawn, Illinois. Plus, taking care of the house was a formidable task for a ninety-one-year-old. His new two-bedroom apartment would be much less stressful, once we helped him settle in, close to us.

But before the new began, his old life would have to end.

As I glanced around the room, I watched all of the fixated expressions on Dad. About fifteen of his neighbors and friends had gathered for a last dinner party to commemorate their friendships. The event at Palermo's

Italian Restaurant, one of Mom and Dad's favorite casual dining establishments, was classy, just like my parents. Dad had paid a little extra for a private room, and I knew everyone appreciated the authentic Italian dishes, garlic bread, salad and scrumptious desserts. Dad and I each had Veal Parmigiana. It was every bit as tender and flavorful as I remembered. Most had brought presents, pictures and other remembrances as a gesture of their long friendships.

Mrs. Baker was there from across the street. I had played with her five kids as we grew up. Mrs. Günter and her daughter, Diane, his next-door neighbors, were there too. Diane had been in my high school class. In fact, I might have asked her out if I hadn't been so awkward with girls back then. She had been married and divorced, as had so many of our classmates. Mrs. Günter and Mrs. Baker were in their eighties. At fifty-eight, I was one of the youngest in the room.

As the evening drew to an end, smiles and heartfelt sentiments were exchanged with an air of finality. Mom would have loved this party.

During the next couple of days, I had too much time to remember the happy, and some not so happy experiences of my youth. I had spent so many holidays there with my parents. It had been my house when I was growing up, but it became Mimi's and Papa's house for our children. With mom gone, it just wasn't the same, but still hard to leave.

When I first saw the brand-new yellow brick ranch house as a five-year-old, a prairie surrounded it, because the sod had yet to be planted. Upon my first walk outside, curious neighborhood kids swarmed me. I had no fear and started making play plans with them.

So much had changed from those first days. The house had its third roof, a number of full-grown trees and the perfect lawn, which dad had meticulously worked on for all of those years. This time was so different. We would be leaving forever.

As we packed, a stream of friends and neighbors stopped by to say goodbye. Most of the women cried or teared up. Everyone emphasized how much Dad would be missed, and how much they already missed Mimi, my mom. Dad was frequently on the verge of tears himself and vowed to visit someday. God willing, I would ensure he fulfilled his promise.

After three days of organizing, packing, visiting and remembering, Friday was upon us. Crystal packed up books, dishes, tablecloths, dolls, toys, photo albums, and more items that we were taking to our house, mainly to give to our daughters. I was amazed at the number and quality of picture albums mom lovingly assembled. I remembered an earlier conversation. I had no interest in looking at them as I grew up. She assured me that someday I would. She was right. That day had come.

Crystal and I separated the furniture Dad would use in his apartment, and gave the rest to a nearby church. We had attended that church when we lived in Chicago, and still had friends there. I joked with the moving men, that people didn't move out of this neighborhood; they died. To some extent, that was true. The Browns across the street died years ago. Mrs. Brown was a real sweetie; Mr. Brown let me sip his beer when I was a ten-year-old kid. Recently, the Byczeks died, within weeks of each other. Their son, Tim, was my best friend as we grew up. Tim and his brother Kevin and sister Karen still lived in the area, and attended Mom's funeral.

When all of the hard work was done, we once again said goodbye to the old house and neighborhood. As Dad and I drove away, the yellow brick building looked the same, but somehow different. Mom and Dad weren't there to wave goodbye. I knew we probably had heard the last of our steps creaking going down to the basement. Never again could I walk barefoot on its thick piled carpeted hardwood floors. Mom and dad would never again fight over the thermostat setting. The wonderful aromas emanating from mom's cooking were just another memory. Without our furniture and Mimi's homey touches, it would never be the same. I watched for as long as I could in the rearview mirror, and then it was on to a new life for Dad.

Dad and I talked a lot during the six-hour trip, mostly remembering people and places, and discussing the numerous details yet to be accomplished. Dad was counting on me. He had always been one of the smartest, best organized people I knew. However, he had lost a step or two physically and mentally during the past couple of years.

I would come through for him as he had for me so many times.

Dad's new apartment was in New Albany, more than an hour away from Warsaw, Ohio where we lived. We stayed at the Hilton at Easton Mall. For the next two days my wife, Crystal, our three daughters, a boyfriend, our son-in-law, and a grandchild helped unpack. On the walls, we hung his favorite landscape paintings and photos. The elegant china cabinet and his blue couch fit nicely into the living room. A bed from their basement was set up in his guest room. Crystal and I stayed an extra night in that room to ensure he was OK.

Once again, it came time to say goodbye. Deep discomfort gripped me as we drove away. I was confident we had done the right thing. Dad was now an hour and fifteen-minute drive away. So why did it feel so wrong?

Seeing Dad wave, alone again was unsettling. This was his choice more than anyone's. He couldn't stay in Oak Lawn without Mom, and needed to be near all of us. Seeing him waving in front of the apartment and not our yellow brick house just wasn't right. However, I felt the same way the first time we drove away from Dad, standing in front of the yellow brick house, without Mom.

My memories of that house, the neighborhood and Mom and Dad, gave me the idea to write this book for our girls and our grandchildren.

Siegfried and Ron Meinstein in front of the yellow brick house, just before move to Ohio, in September of 2012.

A New Home

Construction of our first home was completed during the summer of 1959. The yellow bricks shone in stark contrast to the dark gray shingled roof. I was just five years old and had no idea why we had moved from our Chicago apartment to the corner of Oak Center Drive and Cook Avenue, in Oak Lawn, Illinois. My dad just said the old neighborhood was changing, and he had always planned on a house for his family.

Whatever the reasons, I didn't care. Here we were in a brand-new three-bedroom house, surrounded by houses that didn't look much older. Initially, my favorite feature about the corner brick ranch was the small prairie encircling it. I investigated my new surroundings and dreamed of all of the hours I could spend discovering, and playing with bugs and plants.

Later that summer, I was disappointed when the pretty prairie was converted to another boring lawn, to match the neighborhood. Well, they could take my prairie, but not all of the insects left. I found out why it's not a good idea to catch a honeybee with your bare hands. The bee obviously didn't know he would become the star of a show-and-tell for my mother. My painful life's lesson that day was that, every other creature wouldn't see things the way I did.

Back on that first day at our house, though, I wasn't outside long before the neighborhood kids swarmed me.

The boys and a few curious girls were a variety of ages. I was a little scared, but mostly excited. I had no idea that some of them would soon become the friends of my youth. I would attend school with them, spend endless hours biking, playing sandlot baseball, football—and occasionally getting into trouble—with them.

Another great thing happened that first year. I got my first television set—a hand-me-down from my dad's uncle and aunt. (Notice I said "my TV.") I took to this miracle immediately. Imagine, a device that picked up a signal out of the air (no cables back then) and transformed it to sound and a picture!

If these signals were in the air, then why couldn't we hear or feel them? My fascination with questions like that was probably why I became a scientist.... that plus my great interest in my dad's job managing a chemical lab. Of course, when asked in school what my dad did, I proudly told the class, "He's a chemical." Years later, my first-grade teacher still remembered that, with a smile.

As for the TV, it could have been the prototype. It had a brown furniture box about four feet high by three feet wide and three feet deep, with a ten- or twelve-inch screen in the middle. We could get any of the four stations with a minimum amount of distortion. First, of course, you had to adjust the rabbit ears (inside antenna). I quickly got all too good at it, and spent way too many hours infatuated with this new form of entertainment, just as kids are today with their phones and other electronic devices.

As a boy in the 1960s, I was irresistibly drawn to action programs, particularly cowboys and Indians. That was before the time of politically correct terms.

My favorite show aired right after school—*Garfield Goose and Friends* (or Garfinkle as my mother insisted,

I called him). It was a puppet show hosted by Frazier Thomas, a robust, friendly man. The two most notable puppets were Mr. Rabbit and Garfield Goose, who wore a crown, and went by the title of King of the United States. Garfield Goose could only clap his beak together, and Mr. Rabbit, an apparent mute, would wiggle his nose to feign speech. I loved when they argued, and the omnipresent Mr. Thomas interpreted for them, because naturally, he had no problem understanding or conversing with either one. Their fights inevitably ended with the goose hitting the rabbit's head with his beak, and a subsequent rebuke by Mr. Thomas. This usually segued into a cartoon. My favorite cartoon characters included Bugs Bunny, Daffy Duck, and Mickey Mouse. Adventure shows like "Superman" and the "Lone Ranger" were other early TV favorites. Early television was safe for children to watch when we were inside, and not playing outside. Moms didn't have to worry about bad words or violence on TV, like they do today.

The 50s and 60s

TV watching aside, I was healthy and active. I lived for summers of sandlot baseball, biking, and swimming. Frigid weather ushered in sledding, snowball fights, and skiing with my parents on winter getaways.

Now that I think about it, my high energy was the probable source of a problem in my early schooling. I spent a lot of time looking out the window, daydreaming, when I should have been listening to the teacher. Today, they likely would have diagnosed me with ADD (attention deficit disorder). Back then, kids were just labeled good or bad, plain and simple. Around seventh or eighth grade, I discovered something today's drug companies don't want you to know: You can grow out of it naturally. At least, I think so.

One day, while we were taking turns reading a story written on the board, the teacher noticed I was having trouble. After class, she suggested I have my eyes checked. I did, and lo and behold, I needed glasses. At school, the kids and my teacher said they made me look intelligent. It might have been a coincidence, but soon my grades improved, because I started to find at least some of what the teacher was saying interesting.

Back then, my mother would have declared me the perfect child. My father would have been more realistic, though. One day, I was dribbling the basketball in the basement—against their orders—when I knocked over a dresser and broke off the handles. When I heard my mother walking down to see what happened, I pulled the dresser on top of myself and started moaning. She seemed shocked and concerned just as I'd hoped. I think my acting was exceptional. Bogart had nothing on me. Unfortunately, the basketball three feet away gave me away.

Another time, I climbed up the apple tree in the backyard and waited for Mom to walk under the tree on her way to the clothesline. Then quietly, with my hand over my mouth, I called to Mom a few times. I giggled a little each time she looked around. When she began to look concerned and started to walk around the house to find me, I yelled, "Up here, Mom!" She said something in German, told me I was mean, and ordered me down. I obeyed, but I couldn't stop smiling. She threatened to fetch her fabled wooden spoon, but then gave in when I started back up the tree.

Actually, I was always trying to take advantage of my mother's good nature. She made it too easy. She took her mother role very seriously. I know she and Dad didn't get pregnant easily. When I finally came along, I became her gift from God. That's why she considered me nearly perfect. As any normal kid, I learned to take advantage of her, and she somewhat enjoyed letting me. Home was always a soft place to fall. She treated my friends and I, like royalty.

At five foot three inches, Mom seemed tall in those early days. Her dark brown hair was always perfect, but a little scratchy with hair spray. Her rose red lips sometimes left a slight stain on my forehead when she put me to bed. She usually remedied the problem with a little rub of her thumb. She always wore a nice, usually floral patterned, house dress. As she passed, her dress made a slight rustling sound. She left behind the faint odor of her perfume.

After a hot day on the ball field, she had the Kool-Aid and store-bought cookies (usually Oreos) ready, just like on TV. If my friends were busy, she would take a break from housework (which she also took seriously) to play a game with me, or even go on a bike ride.

My parents were frugal. I'm sure being German and living through the Great Depression were the roots of this. I too learned at an early age: to spend money wisely.

Back then, most stores handed out green stamps (a little smaller than postage stamps) based on how much you purchased. Once you filled a book with them, you could redeem them at a green stamp store for prizes. One book could get you perhaps a bottle opener or an oven mitt. The more books, the bigger the prizes, up to TVs, toasters, mixers and other appliances.

My mom was on a mission to help with the family finances. Her plan—it took me a while to buy in—was to purchase a professional hair-cutting kit, and save money by cutting my hair. I went along with the plan, since it meant an outing with Mom. Besides, I could care less who cut my hair. Furthermore, in my mind, I could transform the savings as more trips to the local pet store. It was one of my favorite places. Not only did I love seeing all of the animals, but the store had several cases filled with penny candy. These colorful and tasty treats included various hard candies, Atomic Fireballs, Bit O Honeys, Turkish Taffy, and even necklaces made out of candy. Most were just one penny, but some, like salted pumpkin seeds were two cents. The most extravagant items, such as the aforementioned necklace or wax lips, went for a solid nickel. So, Mom and I walked the eight blocks to 95th street, and took the bus to the green stamp store in Evergreen Park, Illinois. We turned in 10 books, the stamps she had been saving for the past year.

I was impressed with our prize. The clippers, accompanied by a comb, brush, scissors, and instruction book, looked exactly like my barber's. I can only assume my mother read the book. What the kit was missing, though, was an actual barber. I soon realized why barber colleges exist.

I settled in the kitchen with dish towels draped over me. Mom slowly grazed the noisy electric clippers through my dark brown hair. Eventually, the clippers stopped. She groaned.

I turned around.

She was holding back tears and said something in German.

"What did you do?" I asked.

"I think I got a little close."

Two mirrors divulged that I was now the only first-grader with a bald spot on the back of the head. I jumped up and reacted like Ricky did when Lucy screwed up on TV (minus the Spanish). I stopped acting when Mom started to cry. After all, I didn't care that much about my hair. My act did inspire Mom with a plan.

The next day, I reluctantly dragged myself to school with my dad's black shoeshine polish hiding the bald spot. Nobody noticed except my teacher! She laughed when I told her the story in private. In fact, she couldn't stop laughing. I think I had made her day. I, however, was not as pleased.

It would have been funny enough if the story ended there. But several months later, you guessed it: She wanted to try again. She didn't want to admit she had squandered all those hard-earned green stamps. She was certain that she had figured out what had gone wrong. This time, she would be extra careful.

My hair actually looked more even, and she was almost finished when her hand slipped or my head moved – depending on who you ask.

Out came the shoe polish again.

The next day, I went to school with a rather dubious half eyebrow. I know what you're thinking… I wish I were making this up.

That was the last time I saw the barber kit.

Not every memory of my childhood was that tumultuous. I had a pretty normal childhood. Of course, "normal" back in the sixties was a bit different than it is today. I remember my overprotective mother letting me go out on my own, or with a friend for my Cub Scout fund-raisers, trick or treating, etc. Mothers often were home during the day and usually knew each other, and most of the kids.

When I was twelve, my dad told me that the next-door neighbor's wife had left him, and their two children to be with another man. I couldn't believe it. Married people didn't leave! What about, "till death do us part?" And what about the kids? How could one person raise a kid?

Of course, today it seems that everything has tilted in the other direction. Vows should read, "till something better comes along."

Back then, I felt only slightly insecure when my parents discussed topics loudly and passionately (argued). Rule one for a long marriage is open communication (just kidding). Most of the time, however, we got along well. Whether by design or circumstance, the three of us were mostly alone in the world. We had few close relatives, and outside of talking to the neighbors from our porch, few close relationships.

I didn't appreciate that fact until I met my wife. In Crystal's family, you need a computer program to keep track of friends and relatives.

However, regardless of our relative isolation, I realized early that, you can't shelter yourself from the world.

A Nation Mourns

I believe history builds upon itself. Every major event changes the course of the future, and limits the possible outcomes of future events. For example, if Adolf Hitler had fallen through the ice and died as a youth, Germany and the world would have a different history. This would have impacted you. For example, you probably wouldn't be reading this book right now.

I have vague remembrances of events in the early sixties. During John F. Kennedy's brief presidency from 1961 to 1963, I was impressed with the articulate, charismatic man. I had trouble understanding him, because of his Boston accent, but some terms stuck with me. In particular, "space race" drove my imagination. Just like the *Flash Gordon* TV series, man was going to the moon. What or who would we meet there?

I also remember Bay of Pigs (invasion of Cuba) in 1961. What were all of those pigs doing in the water? Around that time, we had a new drill in school. I had trouble keeping everything straight. For fires, we would go outside. For tornadoes, we would go into the hall or restrooms. In the new one for nuclear attack, we would hide under our desks and close our eyes.

This led to some questions for Mom and Dad. Why did Russia want to bomb us? We were nice, right? I don't remember the answer. It must have been boring.

Crystal never experienced those drills. Apparently, if you lived in Chicago instead of a suburb, you wouldn't have time to get under your desk.

I had no idea that, my questions soon would be replaced with many more. Some events are so dramatic that they not only affect history, but also can impact the basic ideologies and beliefs of large masses of people in an instant. More recently on September 11, 2001, the tragedy now known just as 911 is an example. The terrorist attacks not only affected the people of New York City, and our nation, but also the world. The security of every non-terrorist person on the planet was threatened. If this could happen to the "greatest nation on Earth," who could be safe?

Another event of long-term impact occurred when I was nine. On November 22, 1963, President Kennedy was assassinated in Dallas, Texas. Like 911, everyone can remember what they were doing, and where they were when they heard the news.

I remember sitting in my fourth-grade classroom, looking out the window (yes, daydreaming), waiting for the teacher to return. The principal had summoned all of the teachers to the office a few minutes earlier. My teacher's usual put-together appearance made her return even more dramatic. Dark lines from her eyes ran down her fair skin. Her announcement was short and to the point; "Gather your books and go home. President Kennedy has been shot. I will see you next week."

She disappeared back into the hall, where she tried to compose herself.

As a spoiled, somewhat self-centered nine-year-old, I was elated at the thought of a long weekend… until Mom greeted me at the door.

"Why are you home?" she asked.

Finally, I knew something she didn't! With a pause for dramatic effect, I said, "Haven't you heard? President Kennedy's been shot."

My mother's face flushed. "Oh my God!" She rushed over to turn on the TV. By then, the news was reporting the president was dead.

"Oh my God!" my mom repeated as the reporter talked. "Oh no!" She quietly cried as Walter Cronkite, the stoic face of the news for her generation, continued his report. He also looked on the verge of either crying, or hitting something.

Even though Crystal was a year younger than me, she was more sensitive to world events, and less self-absorbed. Her mother considered it part of her mission to educate her children about world events, pointing out famous people, such as authors, actors, politicians, preachers, or humanitarians, on TV. She never missed a rocket launch.

She taught Crystal and her siblings that, God has a purpose for everything and everybody. The president's assassination tested their faith, though.

Crystal

I remember President Kennedy as being very dynamic and intelligent. Mom said he was the first president we saw on TV, and it was different than the radio and newsreels. His wife, Jackie Kennedy, was beautiful and very fashionable. She was someone to watch. I dressed my Barbie doll in outfits like hers, with matching hats and shoes. We would see their children, Caroline and John-John, playing on the White House lawn, and at the beach.

When President Kennedy died, my mother cried for days. "They shot our president. How could this happen?" she kept saying.

They closed the schools, and everyone was sad. The funeral was on TV for days, and Mrs. Kennedy was dressed in black with a black lace veil over her face. You knew that she was crying. It was terrible and frightening to see. Horses pulled the casket in the procession. I felt very sorry for Caroline and John-John because they had lost their dad. I was crazy about my dad and couldn't imagine losing him.

Immediately after the event, I continued to watch as my mom cried. I did notice some dark spots on Jackie's jacket during Lyndon B. Johnson's emergency swearing in. Years later, I discovered they were specks of her late husband's blood, because she hadn't changed her clothes. I can't even imagine what she must have endured.

LBJ was the opposite of the young and vibrant President Kennedy. He was tall and old, and talked slow with a Southern drawl. But his wife, Lady Bird Johnson, was like a fashionable, friendly grandmother. How could you not like someone named Lady Bird?

The Vietnam War was raging, and the news showed servicemen fighting and dying every day. My mom listened to the casualty reports on our kitchen radio. I wanted the war to end as soon as possible, but it dragged on and on. We were glad that my brother couldn't be drafted because of physical problems. We watched young men in our neighborhood in Dolton, Illinois, leave to fight in Vietnam. Some of them died or came back disabled. It was a very sad time. Ron and I agree that history might have been better if President Kennedy had survived.

Ron

At the time, neither Crystal nor I had any idea what a profound effect the president's death could have on the nation. I was more concerned that, there was nothing else on television. OK, he's dead, why depress us further?

Little did I know that, this was part of a national grieving process, or that things would never be the same. It was the end of an age of innocence. If even our president wasn't safe, how safe were the rest of us?

We had no idea how much the 1960s were heating up, with Vietnam, race issues, gender role issues, etc. The disenfranchised youth rebelled against hypocrisy, and an American value system was under attack.

There was no telling how great of an impact President Kennedy's leadership could have had. Among other things, he was instrumental in pushing America to the lead in the space race. I wish he at least could have seen Neil Armstrong take those first steps on the moon in 1969.

Well, maybe he did. I like to think he had a front-row seat.

The Christmas Package

A more personal example of how the effects of history can linger involved a special delivery from Germany each Christmas. The box always spoiled us with some of the most delectable cookies, candies, and assorted German treats. My favorite was lebkuchen, a soft gingerbread cookie covered with chocolate or a sweet glaze.

Not being the most inquisitive child, I was around ten or eleven before I asked my dad where the boxes came from, and what we had done to deserve them. His answer changed the way I viewed him forever.

My dad never talked much about the war or what he had done. I realize now he was trying to protect my innocence, and he probably thought I wouldn't understand. I'm sure he was right.

For one thing, Siegfried Meinstein wasn't just a soldier during World War II. He was a counterintelligence agent, assigned to an Army infantry division in Germany. While there are jokes that Army intelligence is an oxymoron, the concept of counterintelligence was a little tougher for me to grasp. As I understand it, intelligence is responsible for acquiring and analyzing information to supply strategic information, and suggestions to higher Army staff, to facilitate their planning efforts. Counterintelligence, however, as a division of the intelligence effort, was responsible for acquiring and analyzing information to determine the enemy's strategies. In other words, they needed to get into the enemy's heads. Dad immigrated to America from Germany, to live with his Uncle Max, when he was 13 years old. After he graduated from college, and joined the Army, he excelled in his training and became a counter intelligence officer.

Part of my dad's responsibility as a counterintelligence officer, with the 83rd National Guard unit, was to interrogate prisoners and German persons of interest. As a native German, who spoke the language and was a very intelligent, incisive man, my dad was ideal for that responsibility.

Dad told me that, by the time he arrived, closer to the end of the war, after D-day, many German prisoners, especially those who were "volunteered," had lost faith in the Fluhrer's great plan. They needed little inducement to divulge what they knew.

One such inductee defected by swimming across a river near my dad's unit. (Let's call him Hans, because I never got his name). He surrendered to infantry soldiers, who brought him to my dad for interrogation. After my dad's usual line of questioning, Hans was not only willing, but grateful, to help. They chatted about their shared experiences growing up in the free, pre-Hitler Germany. Their love for their homeland had turned to hatred for how perverted it had become.

Hans made it clear that he hated confinement, and just wanted to return to his family. However, he knew he had to wait until the German threat was over. If he returned before then, he could again be picked up by one of the German "volunteer" wagons, or be killed as a defector.

After a couple of days of Hans's confinement, my dad had an ingenious idea. If Hans was willing to help, and to stay with the unit under supervision, Dad promised he would be released to return to his family as soon as the war was over.

Hans helped with the interrogations—not as an interrogator, but as a German prisoner. When Dad identified a prisoner that he wanted to interrogate, Hans would wear a confiscated German uniform, and be taken under guard, to the interrogation site. Next, the prisoner was brought in and thrown down next to Hans, who would act nervous and start a conversation with the prisoner. Although Dad never told me details, I can imagine what happened. After trying to glean a little information from casually talking, Hans would say something like, "I think I've heard of this Siegfried. He's a German Jew, and will stop at nothing unless we tell him the truth."

Dad would shout, "Bring in the next prisoner!" Guards would drag in Hans, while he struggled. Dad would start off quietly with questions about his unit and troop movements before raising his tone, and eventually shouting and swearing in German. Hans may have pleaded for his life, or said, "I have family."

Finally, Dad would shout, "You have not told me everything you know, so die, you German dog!" He would unholster his sidearm and fire rounds into the ground, a coal bin, etc. The assisting infantry soldiers would decorate Hans with blood saved from the mess tent. Next, they carried Hans's seemingly lifeless body by the awaiting German prisoner. Dad would then shout, "Bring in the next prisoner!"

By this time, the prisoner was as nervous as a cat, and had to be dragged in. Dad told me the interrogation usually was considerably shorter than the mock interrogation, and nearly 100 percent effective. Of that, I have no doubt.

Among Dad's traits, his yelling for effect is unsurpassed. As a kid, I could usually fool Mom, but I spilled everything to Dad. He never threatened to shoot me, but I knew I had something to fear if he raised his voice.

After that first war story from my dad, I appreciated Hans's annual gift boxes all the more. In fact, I still think of him every time I have the opportunity to eat a lebkuchen.

Boy Scouts

My parents lived long enough to become Senior citizens, and they owe it all to me and the Boy Scouts of America.

Mom had a two-pack-a-day cigarette habit, and Dad savored his fat cigars. I still remember coughing and gagging, the sick feeling I used to suffer in the car. Winters were the worst because the car windows were closed. Their smoke had no place to escape to, except in my lungs. Back then, most adults smoked, and the cigarette companies were just starting to lose control over the truth about the dangers of smoking. Second hand smoke was unknown.

I was eleven when I gave my mom an ultimatum: If she would quit smoking, I would never start. Coincidentally, that was my first year of Boy Scout camp. I had never been away from my mother for more than a few hours, let alone for two weeks

I was excited. She was nearly hysterical with fear.

Her one and only baby was leaving, and she couldn't protect him. Actually, I felt sorrier for my dad because of what he'd have to endure during my absence. I'm certain my mom, obsessed over leaving me at camp, must have made some kind of deal with God to protect me from any dangers that were there. She chose that week to stop smoking. Every time I remembered to call her; I could hear it in her quivering voice. She was losing it. But

I could tell she was overjoyed that, I was still alive, and having fun.

When I returned home, she nearly crushed me with a bear hug. True to her word to God, she never picked up another cigarette. Once her sense of smell returned, though, she became painfully aware of the foul odors emanating from Dad's cigars. Dad managed to keep smoking for more than a decade, under the siege of complaints, but finally decided to make the smart choice for health reasons—including mental, I'm sure.

Scouting not only helped my parents, but changed my life. I developed leadership skills, learned a great deal about nature, especially survival in the woods, empathy for younger scouts, and people in general. My journey to becoming an Eagle Scout was difficult, but exciting. I believe those experiences helped me to make better decisions, and take on difficult challenges. This has helped me in my educational endeavors, family life, and various careers.

My daughters appreciate that I understand nature, cooking, camping, and reading maps. When they were dating, they looked for guys who were in Scouting. I'm also well versed in a variety of subjects, which I attribute partly to Scouting.

Scouting teaches skills such as self-sufficiency, teamwork, and leadership. However, it's just plain fun too.

The eight hours on a school bus to Boy Scout camp always seemed to last forever, but it was worth it when we arrived in the middle of the huge, forested area, in central Michigan. Our troop was one of roughly thirty that shared the 4800-acre Camp Owasippe Scout Reservation campgrounds, north of Muskegon, Michigan. Two weeks wasn't even enough time to accomplish all the activities—working on merit badges, competitions, hikes, swimming, canoeing, canoe races, obstacle courses, etc.

One year when I was fifteen, and had achieved a rank of Life Scout, the troop leaders separated us into three groups for a compass hike. The Scoutmaster and Assistant Scoutmaster led the first two, and asked me to lead the third group. Each group was given a map and a compass, plus supplies. We would start from the same point at different times. The goal was to a reach a specific lake, and meet the other groups by dusk. Once there, we were to set up camp for the night, and return the next day. This was a big honor for me, and a chance to apply what I had learned.

I discussed the ten-mile route with senior members of our eight-man group. As on any true compass path, we walked cross-country and made beelines lining up a near tree to one in the distance, along the compass path. However, no one had ever explained how difficult this could be in a thick forest.

About two miles in, we came across a hunter's path running roughly the same direction. It took little convincing to follow it. After another hour, we ate our bag lunches and continued. By late afternoon, we still hadn't recognized anything on the map. One of the tired younger Scouts started crying. I reassured him we would be fine, and that we'd hike just a little farther. Leaders sometimes have to sound confident when they're not.

I estimated that we had walked between twelve and sixteen miles when we discovered a clean little lake, with a sandy beach big enough to set up camp. It wasn't the lake we were hiking to meet with the other groups, but it was time to make camp. Scouting teaches you to be adaptable. We started fires and boiled water for the dehydrated meals. After dinner, we stripped to our shorts and played in the lake for a couple of hours until dark. A conveniently fallen log made for a great game of king of the log.

The next morning after a bountiful breakfast of green eggs and ham (no reference to Dr. Seuss, but dehydrated eggs can have a green tint), we took the hunter's path to a road and eventually made it back to camp. I listened as the young Scout, who had cried, told everyone about our grand adventure. I felt like I had failed by not finding the right lake, but then felt reprieved when I learned that it had eluded the Scoutmasters as well.

My lesson? Don't lose it when you're lost. Everyone gets lost at some point, whether it's physically or mentally. You can either choose to get upset, or accept the experience for what it is—an opportunity to discover something new, and perhaps even better.

I also learned an important cliché in Scouting: You never fail until you quit trying.

Skiing

While I enjoyed team sports, my absolute favorite activity was skiing. My parents learned in Europe, and we went at every opportunity.

I tried on my mother's skis when I was eight, the best age to learn. They didn't fit right, but I didn't care. On my first attempt at the bunny hill I probably fell down at least ten times, and another five going up on the tow rope. The great thing about learning young is being close to the ground. And once I learned how to get up, I didn't have a long way to go.

Skiing felt like entering a new world, a part of nature. It's hard to describe the freedom. I decided where I wanted to go on the slope, and how I wanted to get there. It fed my senses: the cool breeze, the sights and sounds of the great outdoors, and the smell of pines. I also met some of the nicest people on the lifts.

On weekends, we usually skied at Chicago area resorts, such as Wilmot or Alpine Valley, just over the Wisconsin border. During Christmas vacation, we often ventured to nice resorts in further up in Wisconsin or Michigan, including the Upper Peninsula. On Christmas day, the slopes were all but empty. No lines.

Most people spent Christmas with family, but we were our family. My dad had relatives in New York and Florida, but my mom's were in Germany.

My dad and I would enjoy the slopes all day, though we seldom skied together. I liked to zip down a little faster than he did. Occasionally, I would find my mom on one of the easier slopes or in the lodge. She never liked the cold, and it didn't like her. Her hands would turn the most disturbing shade of blue with limited exposure. She was also afraid of falling, which made it hard to improve. She did get better with my help, but I think what she liked most was spending time with me. When it was frigid, she spent most of the day in the lodge by the fire. She didn't seem to mind, as long as we came in frequently to warm up, and took her out for a nice dinner.

We usually returned home around New Year's. The next morning, Santa had come, like magic. I had to open my presents fast, though, so we could move on to New Year's. Being the only child had its perks, especially at Christmas. My mother tried her best to spoil me, and I didn't fight it. The tree had more presents than would fit under it. Those were great times.

I was seventeen when we took one of my most memorable ski trips. My dad decided to go all out over Easter break, and splurge on Breckenridge, Colorado. It was unbelievably beautiful. Nothing can match skiing in snow-covered mountains. It must have been about a thousand feet down to the tree line. We could ski trails up to six miles long, and I took frequent breaks to savor the view. Also, I needed to catch my breath, because of the thin air at the high elevations (up to 12,000 ft.).

I also had to catch my breath at lower elevations, where girls skied in bikinis. There was a substantial temperature difference between the top and the bottom of the mountain. At the top, it could be thirty degrees with powder blowing everywhere, but warmer, in the fifties at the bottom. I was told girls in bikinis skied for free.

Another memorable trip was to upper Michigan, where I distinctly remember my last run on the last day. I had taken full advantage of the resort, and had skied almost all day on my favorite runs. I rode one of the last chairs of the day to the highest point, and took my time, enjoying the scenery one last time as I descended. I was probably still several hundred feet up when I spotted my mom by one of the ski racks at the lodge.

I could always pick her out because of her outfit, which was the warmest, fluffiest, bright florescent orange snowsuit. From a distance, she reminded me of a bright-orange tennis ball. She was terrified of being lost in the snow. Well, I think a commercial airliner probably could have spotted her!

I decided to head in her direction, when I noticed I was the last skier on the slope. I really loved going fast, and feeling like I was flying, with the wind rushing against my face. I was on a rather bumpy mogul type of run, and schussing (skiing straight down), for safety reasons, was discouraged. As the last one on the slope, I knew I would be the only one in danger. So I took a few deep breaths and kicked off hard.

Before long, I was flying down the hill, my legs acting like shock absorbers. They dropped over each bump and jammed into my chest as I hit the next one. As I neared the bottom, my eyes were tearing, even inside my mask. I could still see the orange ball, though. The lodge was over a small dry creek bed and up about a fifteen to twenty-foot embankment.

As I reached the bottom, I knew I couldn't stop safely before the creek, so I decided to jet up the embankment as far as I could. After I flew over the creek and hit the embankment, though, I didn't seem to slow down much. As I shot up, I decided to continue all the way to the lodge and use my usual skid stop. If I had enough speed, I'd dust my mom with a little snow. I told you, I lived to scare her.

At the top of the embankment, I still had enough speed to send me airborne for a second. Even with eyes full of tears, I could still make out the big orange ball, the target of my tyranny. My evil plan would have worked except for one little detail.

As my skis hit the snow, my mom was still thirty to forty feet in front of me. I looked down and noticed the ground changed from white to brown about fifteen feet ahead. Before I could react or even contemplate my fate, my skis stopped dead. As they flew off, my safety straps broke, and I did my best Superman imitation. Unlike the man of steel, however, I dropped like a rock and started sliding, bouncing, and rolling. The next thing I knew, I was on the ground faceup looking at my mom.

"Hi, Mom," I said.

That's when she realized that the maniac, she had been watching was me.

After reverting to her native German for a few syllables, she put her hands to her face. "Are you OK?"

"OK, I think."

"Are you crazy? Are you trying to kill me?"

"Nah, just having a little fun."

After assessing my bumps and bruises, I gathered up my skis and we looked for Dad in the lodge.

That evening, the main topic was, "What were you thinking?" And secondly, "Were you thinking at all?"

My mother conjured up twenty to thirty possible tragic outcomes which could have befallen me, her, or us.

Despite that day, I skied into young adulthood, but then less and less, after I almost killed Crystal a few times (her words, not mine). My parents continued to ski well into their sixties, and Mom always told the story about the nut, who flew down the slope, and turned into her son at her feet.

Dad taking my skis out of the ski rack.

Showing off my form.

My mother in her famous bright orange snowsuit.

Crystal's Childhood

Crystal

I was born on June 29th, 1955 in Chicago. (Note from Ron to husbands: If you ever forget your wife's birthday, just stab yourself in the heart. It's quicker.)

Ron found it interesting how I got my name, Crystal. While I have been addicted to the same two TV soap operas for a long time, my mom first listened to them on the radio. My name, Crystal, came from one of my mom's favorite soap opera characters, Crystal Carpenter, a very sweet blue-eyed blonde, on *As the World Turns*. *The Young and the Restless*, and *Guiding Light* also entertained us for many years.

Until I was ten, I grew up in the south Chicago neighborhood of Roseland, close to where my father grew up. Immigrants from Sweden, Germany and Lithuania founded Roseland in the mid-1800s. Before it was named, a thoughtful husband planted rosebushes in their backyard to please his wife. When the other wives spied the beautiful blooms in the spring and summer, they asked their husbands to do the same for them. Eventually, people from other neighborhoods would drive through to see the lovely flowers. Hence, the name Roseland.

My older brother, Larry, and younger sister, Jeannette, and I loved growing up around different accents and traditions. The neighbors were close, friendly and caring. Everybody watched over the children, and mom spoiled new or sick neighbors with her homemade baked goods, a casserole or soup.

I remember falling down in front of a neighbor's house and the owner rushing out to pick me up. He was an Italian man with a beautiful garden. He bandaged my knee, and showed me his flowers and plants in his backyard to coax me to stop crying.

Each day before my dad arrived home from work, mom would change her clothes, brush her dark-brown pageboy hair, and glide on red lipstick. Dad always greeted mom with a hug and a kiss when he walked through the door. We would run over to him, but mom would say, "Let your father read the mail first."

Sometimes mom would perch on the front porch steps or play with us while we waited for dad. She would turn the jump rope that was attached to the house, and I would show off with handstands, leaning my feet against the house.

Love to Read

Literature was important to mom, and she would read poetry to us when we were sick or upset. Her favorites were Robert Frost, Emily Dickinson, Edna St. Vincent Millay, Edgar A. Guest, and Elizabeth Barrett Browning. She referred to the authors as if they were her friends.

The programming worked. Jeannette and I blossomed into avid readers at an early age. Mom asked us to read her favorite classics, including: *Little Women, Jane Eyre, Wuthering Heights,* and *Gone with the Wind.* I loved discussing the books with my mom. When we reached high school, mom complained to our teachers about the books we were reading, such as *The Catcher in the Rye,* and reprimanded them for excluding Charles Dickens, Willa Cather, and Mark Twain. This literature was timeless. Many of my girlfriends didn't read classics. When I was ten, my mother gave me *Rebecca of Sunnybrook Farm.* I still have the book, and its vocabulary is way above the 5th grade level. I loved that book and *A Little Princess.*

My grandmother bought me *Five Little Peppers and How They Grew.* I felt so sorry for the mom in the *Five Little Peppers* book, because she had to recycle thread for sewing. They were so poor, yet the children made a cake for their mom with what they scrounged together. They put raisins in the cake, which struck me as so different from the cakes we made in the 1960s. My grandmother Carlson said she preferred going to bed with a book instead of a doll when she was a child. Even today, I always have a pile of books by my bed.

When I was very young, Pearl S. Buck was on a TV talk show, and mom held me up in front of the set and told me, "This is Pearl S. Buck. She's a wonderful author."

My parents' bookcase overflowed from floor to ceiling in the front hallway of our white frame house. After I learned to read in the first grade, I would stand there and read the book titles. I believed I would be very smart after I read most of them. At eight, I read *The Wonderful Wizard of Oz* to Jeannette, who was four. We would sit on the end of the bed each day and read a chapter. We discussed the story and studied the illustrations.

My father was also a reader. He gave me Dale Carnegie's *How to Win Friends and Influence People* when I was ten. He also recommended Rudyard Kipling's poetry, and Norman Vincent Peale's *The Power of Positive Thinking*. My dad and those authors influenced me on how to deal with people and life.

My parents read to us from a variety of sources, including the *Chicago Daily News*, magazines, the Bible, and books. My mother often handed out articles to us about our interests. She even mailed published articles she found in magazines to friends, and family members, when she wrote them. Some of her letters were twelve pages long. She bought boxes of cards to mail out all year long, so the card companies and post office relied on her.

As if that weren't enough literary influence, my grandma on my dad's side, Dorothy Carlson, would discuss literature, and talked me into taking typing and shorthand classes. Grandma Carlson loved novels by Charles Dickens; and *Sister Carrie* by Theodore Dreiser was her favorite book. I think this was because Grandma Carlson and her sister traveled across the country as stenographers. Sister Carrie went to Chicago to forge an independent life and work in the city. Chicago was my grandmother's favorite city.

Grandma Dorothy Carlson and Grandpa Carlson holding Crystal and Larry on Easter, 1956 at our Roseland house.

While at Bradley University, I told my grandma the novels I was reading for my classes, so we could discuss them. Ron now understands why I majored in English. As much as he hates to admit it, my propensity for the written word has been a good influence on him. Before he met me, he only read when teachers forced him. Now he reads for pleasure, because I brainwashed him, and keep giving him books.

I have always been good at keeping in touch. I exchanged letters with my mom, Jeannette, my grandmother, my Aunt Joann, my friend Debbie, and other relatives, and friends during my two years at Bradley University. Now I not only send cards, but also design them. Some are three-dimensional art that can be displayed. I also craft birthday and Christmas presents, such as crocheted clothing, afghans, quilted wall hangings, dolls and bears. Nobody can say that we don't support the postal system.

Cooking and Holidays

One thing at which Ron is probably better than me, is cooking. It came down to survival when he went away to Bradley University. He hadn't realized what a good cook his mom was until he had to force down all of those cafeteria meals.

He impressed me at the beginning of our relationship with his cooking. Grandma Carlson spent many years cooking for her family, and told me to hang on to Ron. In fact, she had advised both my sister Jeannette and me, to marry men who could cook.

Don't get me wrong, I knew how to cook. I cooked a lot while growing up. When I was twelve years old, my mom spent a lot of time in the hospital. She would call me in the morning and direct me what to defrost from the freezer. Then she would help me plan the meal.

I come from a family of bakers on both sides. On mom's side, we have my great Grandma Frieda Johnson who baked apple pies, efilskeefers (Danish donut holes), cookies, cakes and more goodies. My grandma, Marian Johnson, baked brownies, banana bread, pumpkin, mincemeat and apple pies, and cakes. My Aunt Carol made some wonderful almond cookies, cakes, etc. to feed her five children, and often times us. My Grandma Marian Johnson, cooked most meals for mom, and her siblings, and relatives living in her house. When mom first learned to cook, she made enough for six or more people. After she married my dad, he convinced her, he couldn't eat so much food. Mom Began my cooking education by allowing me to stir the chocolate pudding, when I was in preschool. She would give me a spoon and a bowl to play with in the high chair, letting me taste the pie crust, cake and cookie batter and frosting. Jeannette and I would help flatten the sugar cookies with a sugar-coated glass when we were probably four or five years old.

Holidays were big in my family. Decorations like balloons, streamers and homemade posters were common, as well as special foods and traditions. The whole family participated by either making and displaying decorations, cooking, baking cookies, cakes or other sweets, or organizing activities. Mom, Jeannette, and I did most of the planning and all the cooking, but my Dad and Larry helped with setting up chairs and tables, and running errands. Even our friends would get roped into helping if they were around. My parents were also very outgoing and invited neighbors, friends, and relatives to our celebrations. I was used to these types of family activities, but it took Ron awhile to adjust. He, of course, was instantly enlisted to help. When my mom found out about his cooking skills, she assigned him dishes to make for us. Birthdays, anniversaries, Valentine's Day, St. Patrick's Day and more holidays were celebrated by my family. I remember my mom saying to us "Happy (whatever day it was)" with a big smile and a hug, making our lives seem a little happier and more fulfilling.

Ron used to find all of this a bit ridiculous. He once asked my mom if we were celebrating National Pickle Week. She hit him lightly on the arm. Mom appreciated his sense of humor. After a while, Ron realized that our celebrations of birthdays and holidays were fun. He could tell that a lot of love and caring went into the preparations. My mom was made for holidays. She celebrated life all year long.

There was one celebration in particular that I have never forgotten: I woke up to a bright sunny day when I turned five. I'm sure my mom made something special for breakfast, such as French toast or pancakes. At the party, my friends filled our backyard and played games. I opened presents, and blew the candles out on my angel food cake with chocolate frosting, which my mom made from scratch. She was a great baker, and known throughout the neighborhood for her chocolate chip cookies; Texas chocolate and buttermilk coffee cakes; apple, rhubarb custard, blueberry, butterscotch meringue (Dad's favorite) and lemon meringue pies.

After the party, I was standing in front of our house when my brother's friend raced down the sidewalk, and slammed his head into mine. I fell to the ground and screamed in pain, but I couldn't hear my voice.

The next thing I remember was waking up in the hospital underneath an X-ray machine. I also remember my parents keeping me awake with puppets when I wanted to go to sleep. My mom said I had a concussion for days. As a parent of three girls, I now understand how frightened they must have been. I also realize how much they always loved me, and showed me love. My parents made holidays special for us, but they also made everyday events meaningful.

As a little girl in Roseland, I used to swing in the evening in the backyard. I would pump my legs hard and swing as high as I could as the sun slipped behind the tall poplar trees in the prairie, that I could see from my yard. I remember a feeling of complete happiness. I was safe.

I was loved not only by my parents, brother, sister and friends, but also by God. I was grateful to God for my life. I still am.

In an essay about his life in the seventh grade, my brother wrote that he didn't remember being alive without me, and that we were always together, until he went to kindergarten. I'm sure I was upset when he went to school without me.

But then came my first year of school. I walked with Larry and his friends and my friend, Debbie Bailey, one mile to school. We walked home for lunch, and then back to school. My brother wasn't used to looking after me, and our mom made him hold my hand when we crossed the streets. One day, I waited for him outside the kindergarten door for lunch as usual, but he never showed up. I figured he forgot me, so I finally walked home.

When I arrived, my mother was relieved to see me. I know she was mad at Larry and worried too. Who was holding my hand when I crossed the streets? Needless to say, he didn't forget me again.

When my sister started school, I walked with her and my friends, and held her hand to cross the streets. We were close, and I always took care of her. Larry ignored us and ran off with his friends.

One day when walking home for lunch, I was talking to my friends, and felt like I had forgotten something. Then I realized I wasn't holding Jeannette's hand. I had left her at school!

I ran back as fast as I could. The teacher was with her, and Jeannette was crying hysterically. We hugged, and I coaxed her to stop crying until we got home. Then she cried while our mom held her.

She's never stopped telling that story, and I always remind her that I ran back for her, unlike Larry who just ate lunch without me. But that never seems to matter. As the youngest, she never had the opportunity to forget a sibling at school. I was the one forgotten and who forgot. Such is the fate of the middle child.

My parents liked hosting company and visiting their friends, so people and conversations filled our lives. This gave us a broader view of life and more empathy. If anyone needed help, my parents were always there.

Jeannette and I baked with mom, and distributed the treats to the neighbors. Coming home to warm cookies, cake or pie was common in our house. We frequently tried new recipes from a shelf of cookbooks.

The neighborhood was changing, though. The little multicultural neighborhood of Roseland was spiraling toward gangs and violence. So, we moved south to Dolton, a suburb of Chicago, when I was ten. Our brown three-bedroom brick ranch house was where I was still living when Ron met me

My mom soon joined a homemakers group, and learned interesting things from the women, such as crocheting (which she taught me and Jeannette), embroidery on burlap strips, and how to make bread flowers.

They also taught her the secret to storing clothes when you can't iron them immediately. She would sprinkle clean clothes with water, roll them, and stash them in the freezer to be ironed when she had time, which Ron thought was hysterical. My mom would send me downstairs to the freezer to fetch the clothes. I found this odd and funny, but we dared not question the wisdom of the homemakers group.

I couldn't believe it when a Scottish lady in the group gave the moms recipes using handfuls of flour, and pinches of spices, instead of cups and teaspoons. This reminds Ron of learning his mother's recipes. His mom would describe what the dough should look like, instead of giving measurements. This drove Ron crazy until he did it a few times. As a chemist, he was embarrassed to say, he still doesn't use measuring cups, or spoons for many of his recipes. Our girls hate that. I guess it's the circle of life.

God Has Many Houses

Ron and I both believe; my family exemplified the loving family that today's politicians refer to when hailing family values. My father hugged me, and told me that he loved me, every day that I lived at home, until I was twenty.

My mother was equally affectionate, and always wished us a good day when we left the house. When we returned, she asked us how our day went, and how we felt. It didn't matter if we were angry or sad. She listened and didn't judge us, which I felt helped tremendously. My mom's sense of humor served to lighten life. During dinner, my dad related the funny things that happened at the office, and the jokes he'd heard.

This outlook, while encouraging, was somewhat deceptive. When I started working in his office to make money for college, I discovered my dad's work wasn't nearly as much fun as I had imagined. I realized it was all in my dad's attitude. I think all of us could learn a lesson from that.

My parents' ability to laugh at themselves, and at life, taught us to be more positive. Even during the dark days and hard times, we could find something to laugh about. We also believed in the power of prayer, and the words of the Bible.

Mom often said, "This too shall pass" when things were hard; she would say, "Often life isn't fair, but God is good", and "Our ship will come in." This wouldn't have meant as much if she hadn't been a happy person most of the time. Her smile and laughter made for a happy home. She was also a great problem-solver, and taught us how to brainstorm and to search for answers. She networked with her friends and family to find solutions. Sometimes the answer was just to wait and pray. "God's timing isn't always our timing."

Religion was an important part of our week. In Roseland, we attended the Dutch Reformed Church, which my dad and my Aunt Carol had attended as children. This church was part of a rather strict, legalistic denomination.

My grandfather was Swedish, and had been raised in the Lutheran Church; and my grandmother was a Presbyterian. Although they didn't attend the Dutch Reformed church, they sent their children there because it was in the neighborhood. Once again, score one for location, location, location.

As a young child, I loved the church. Its emphasis was that Jesus loves and cares about all of us. Sunday school was in the basement, where we would march and sing. The teachers were dedicated to mentoring, and taught us Bible verses before we could read. The teachers would give the kids anything they needed, including winter coats, boots, hats, etc. At Christmas, every child received a pound of chocolate candy wrapped in Christmas paper.

The adults in the church, however, seemed to be focused on the message of sin and hell. They never seemed too happy walking out of service. Every Sunday, my parents would debate whether to go. Dad didn't want to attend anymore, but Mom insisted that we needed to go to church. Mom won the argument. Back then, switching denominations wasn't as prevalent as today, so we kept going.

After we moved to Dolton in 1965, we looked for another church, and found a loving, positive Methodist denomination in Sandridge Methodist Church. Twelve years later, in 1978, Ron and I were married by Reverend Bonebrake in Faith United Methodist Church, which was the combination of Sandridge and two other local churches. He was much nicer than his name sounds.

Welcome to Kenosha

Crystal

I remember visiting my Aunt Joann's house in Kenosha, Wisconsin, when Ron and I were newlyweds. This was the same house where mom grew up.

Ron asked me, 'why can't we just rent a motel room?' I told him the same thing I had been told for years by my mom and dad. "When in Rome, do as the Romans do." He learned very quickly that in Rome, or rather Kenosha, my Aunt Joan was Caesar. Ron and I, along with my brother and cousin, Kathy, wound up sleeping on quilts on the dining room floor. At any rate, it was obvious to Ron from day one, that in Kenosha, Aunt Joan was in charge. Mom's younger sister (by six years) was well organized, results oriented, and a caring person (though you couldn't prove it by Ron). If you disagreed with Aunt Joann, which Ron mistakenly did sometimes, you were either wrong or misinformed. He preferred to be misinformed.

Family was everywhere in Kenosha. For Ron, it was definitely culture shock. After having grown up with just his mom and dad, he was now in a position where he couldn't even keep everyone straight. My immediate family was simple enough. Aunt Joan was married to an easygoing and friendly man named Dale. Their children were Kathy, Kim, and Roger. Ron got along great with them. From there it got hazy, with cousins, aunts, uncles, great this, grand that, and also neighbors and friends who visited Aunt Joann's house often. I was accustomed to a lot of people coming in and out of my house in Dolton, but Ron wasn't. My memories of growing up with this American extended family "almost" made Ron jealous.

I remember as a young child, going with my cousin, Kathy, to Great Grandma Frieda Johnson's house, located across the street, and around the corner from Aunt Joan's house. We always found her in the kitchen, often in front of the big black stove. Great Grandma was a short woman, less than five feet tall. with her white hair wrapped around her head in a large braid, and blue eyes like my mom's. She wore flowered house dresses, usually covered by an apron, and sensible, manly looking brown shoes. Great Grandma Johnson would smile at us, ask us questions about everything going on, and gave us samples like cookies or apple pie. She was the only person who ever called me "Mary's girl". I could tell that she was proud of me, and that she loved my mom very much.

Aunt Joann's white frame one and a half story house, where mom, Aunt Helen and Uncle Cliff grew up, was where everyone ate and visited. My sister Jeannette, my cousins and I played in the old musty basement, and the back yard, and on the large enclosed front porch (another place Ron slept a couple of times). The house was usually full of people and activity. My grandmother knew how to get the most out of a very small kitchen, and so did Aunt Joann. At dinner time, everyone squeezed into the too small dining room. Eventually a back room was added, off of the dining room, and the children's table would be set up in there. Ron and I were still considered to be children, even though we were adults.

When my Grandma was still alive, she had a large parrot in a cage in the living room. He talked to us, but said everything backwards. In the morning, he would say "Good Night" and at night, he would say "Good Morning". He said "Goodbye" when anyone entered the room, and "Hello" when they left. We learned quickly not to put our fingers in the cage, because he was a biter.

Grandma was Irish, and very strict. She seemed to have iron clad rules about everything. Fortunately, my brother, sister and I knew how to follow rules. Regardless of her strict household, she obviously loved us. She would put our coloring pictures up on the French doors, that separated the living room from the hallway. She also baked cookies, brownies, pies and cakes, which I always enjoyed. She made doll clothes for Kathy and my baby dolls. She also made some clothes for me. She gave me my first doll, Charley Ann, a life size hard plastic baby doll, that drank and wet. All of our daughters and grandchildren have played with Charley Ann.

In the backyard at Grandma's, there were rows of raspberry bushes. In the morning, she would shove Kathy and me out the back door, with a basket, to pick some for everyone's breakfast. We have a large raspberry patch in our backyard today. The raspberries are everbearing, so friends and neighbors also pick with us. It reminds me of my childhood.

I remember sleeping in my Uncle Cliff's (mom's younger brother) room upstairs, underneath a quilt, feeling the hand stitching and embroidery, in the dark. In the morning, through the window, I could see the beautiful white apple tree blossoms, which fell like snowflakes in the spring.

Growing up, we went to Grandma's house in Kenosha for Thanksgiving, and sometimes for Christmas. My Aunt Joann and Uncle Cliff and cousins, Peggy, Pam and Paul came, as well as my Aunt Helen and Uncle Tom, and cousins, Jimmy, John, Jane and Julie. As the oldest girls, Kathy and I helped with the little ones. All the relatives came ranging from babies to great grandparents. Neighbors visited frequently. There was continuous hugging and comments on how big my brother, sister and I were getting.

One of my fondest early memories, when I was little, was being passed in an almost never-ending chain from lap, to lap, to lap, and ending up on Daddy's, before being tucked into bed. That's Ron and my idea of family.

My own quilts include one which, I fashioned after the view I remember from grandma Marian's attic, appropriately titled "Grandma's Attic" quilt. I also wrote the following poem to be displayed with the quilt.

An Apple Blossom Memory

In this old apple tree sat I before and again
building experiences, which faded like the
melting snow into a river of memory.

And yet as the apple blossoms twirl aimlessly to
the ground, one past sitting becomes as clear as
the cloudless sky.

Scaling the trunk, I had reached my branch and
hid secretly on the day of my seventh Easter.

Company came and went without my presence
for I was as shy as a kitten.

I could not purr happily before a crowd of
strangers,

whose only wishes were either to compliment or
criticize.

Embarrassed by one and hurt by the other, I
dreaded both and fled to hide in my refuge.

Now and then I peeked out to see glimpses of thin
flowered dresses, ribboned straw hats and the
relations beneath them.

Leaning over to eavesdrop I bumped heads with
supposedly another curious refugee.

"What are you doing here?" we said together and
giggled happily, sharing a secret.

And as the apple blossoms glide gracefully to the
ground, I see one as myself and another as my
cousin,

Lying gently side-by-side on the prickly grass
underneath the warm April sun, waiting for the
recurrence of that day.

—Crystal Ann Meinstein

Written in 1973 when I was a Senior in high school, this poem describes my grandmother's house in Kenosha, Wisconsin where I spent many Thanksgivings, Easter vacations and weeks in the summer. My cousin Kathy and I rode bikes, roller skated and played games. My grandmother died when I was seven years old. My Aunt Joann and Uncle Dale moved into her house, and lived there until my Uncle died in 1984. The house was in the family for 90 years. When my older girls were small, I made a quilted wall hanging for a contest. The quilt shows an attic room in my grandmother's house with a cat on top of a trunk, a fan quilt, an antique chair, and a green sewing basket. Through the window you can see the apple blossoms. This fabric was given to me by my mom from my grandmother's house, and was used for the backing of the quilt.

This quilt was embroidered, appliqued, reverse appliqued, pieced and quilted by hand. The fan quilt was made separately and then sewn on. The flooring is Sachiko quilted.

Great Grandma Frieda Johnson, Kenosha, Wisconsin.

1967

Ron

Sometimes major events seem to stop time. Indeed, certain memories linger for the rest of our lives, such as a couple of events in 1967.

While snow in Chicago was hardly unprecedented and removal efforts were fairly effective back then, January 26 was to be different. I ate breakfast on a snowy Thursday morning with predictions up to four inches. No big deal. I walked the three blocks to Sward Elementary School, cutting across the park as usual to save time.

As a twelve-year-old, I loved snow and was excited when I looked out the window. I envisioned snowball fights, and maybe a ski trip with my parents during the weekend.

By the time school let out, it was still snowing hard. I guessed that at least eight to ten inches had accumulated, but it was hard to tell, because the wind had sculpted a number of high snowdrifts. It took maybe an extra fifteen minutes to get home, because I played in the snow with friends.

Once home, I conducted my great shake-off ritual—similar to wet dogs—on the front porch and in the hallway. My mom said the forecast was calling for a couple more inches. My dad told us quite a story, when he arrived home several hours late. Apparently, the normally good Chicago drivers were sliding, causing multiple fender benders, and traffic jams. Several cars had already been abandoned.

The forecast never seemed to change from "two more inches." Were the weathermen stranded at home?

It continued to snow about an inch per hour until ten o'clock the next morning. I was elated that school was canceled—quite the rarity in those days. I lived for adventures like this!

During the next couple of days, we built snow forts and declared war with snowball fights. Plus, I made a lot of money shoveling walkways in the neighborhood. I might have cleared eight or maybe ten bucks. That's a lot of penny candy.

However, reality arose when we ran low on food. So, my dad and I relied on my sled to plough through the three quarters of a mile to the grocery store. Surprisingly, the main road of 95th Street gave us no relief. We trudged down the middle of the four-lane road, passing by car-shaped snow mounds.

When we finally reached the snow-covered parking lot and store, I was amazed to find we weren't alone. In fact, people appeared to be stocking up for the rest of the winter! Shelves were nearly bare—not one loaf of bread. Even the disgusting pumpernickel was gone.

Using his survival skills from World War II, and the Depression, my dad grabbed a couple of bags of rye flour. Several hours later, nothing had ever tasted quite as good as my mother's rye bread. I don't think she even had a recipe. Homemade bread was a staple where she grew up. Sometimes disasters can bring families together.

The snowstorm turned out to be the worst in Chicago history, with up to twenty-three inches after twenty-nine hours. The wind blew the snow into ten-foot drifts. Fifty thousand cars were abandoned on roads and highways, and many people were stranded when the buses and trains stopped. Mail service and food trucks didn't run for several days. Sixty-eight people died, many of them from heart attacks while shoveling the heavy snow. Mayor Richard Daley declared Chicago a disaster area, and asked people to communally shovel the snow in their neighborhoods.

Crystal

The big snowstorm separated our family.

Jeannette and I walked home for lunch on January 26. I had to drag and carry my seven-year-old sister through chest-high snow drifts. At first, I was excited about the snow, but then a little disappointed when Mom said we weren't going back to school. I liked school, especially because it was in a park.

A couple of hours later, my dad called to report he was stranded at his work. He ended up spending the next four days at coworkers' houses, and helped numerous people start the long, arduous process of digging out. It took him several days to get to Dolton, because of all the road closings.

At home, our television broke on the first day. While this was hard for my mom, she was her usual cheerful self. We played in the snow the next several days, but Larry and I had to shovel the front sidewalk, porch, and back sidewalk every two hours to keep it all clear. Mom was ready with dry clothes, snacks, and hot cocoa when we came in.

Like Ron, Larry and I also pulled our wooden sled about six blocks down the middle of a four-lane highway to the grocery store, with nearly bare shelves. My mom kept staples such as flour, sugar, and margarine for baking, so we just needed a few things like milk and eggs to survive the next couple of days.

I still remember the look on Mom's face when she saw the snowdrift touching the garage roof. She threatened to kill us if we tried to climb up there. We didn't dare, and warned our friends.

When my dad finally returned home Sunday, he solved our biggest problem. He and I took our sled to a neighbor's house and borrowed their extra TV.

The next order of business was shoveling out the alley. Our car, like many others, was stuck in the garage. Dad organized family—including Uncle Clary and my cousins, Bobby, David, and Dorothy—and neighbors for a massive neighborhood dig-out. To make the work seem to go faster, there were hints of having snowball fights, making tunnels and snowmen, and sledding with our cousins and friends. These all came to fruition during the next several days.

It's amazing what can happen when a family and/or a community work together. While it was hard work, I was glad to spend time with my dad.

Ron

The second big event of 1967 was a true tragedy. I was riding my bike through a nice subdivision from my Boy Scout meeting around 5:30 p.m., April 21, when I looked up from Henry—my frequently abused, balloon-tired bike—and spotted a tornado in the distance. I felt proud that I recognized the distinctive form, which we had been warned about in school. No, this definitely was not just a triangle-shaped cloud. I looked down at my bike and said, "Look, Henry, a tornado." As it appeared to veer off, I focused on pedaling the last mile, anticipating dinner.

Before I could make it home, though, it started to hail. I was glad I had listened to my mom and wore a light jacket. The quarter-inch hail stung the back of my neck. It probably only lasted about fifteen or twenty seconds, but was quite annoying. In addition to the stinging, the sound the ice pellets made on the street reminded me of machine gun fire in a war movie. Undaunted, I continued riding. As quickly as it had started, the banging of the hail gave way to the eeriest silence. It was too quiet, not even a trace of a breeze. Except for my bike squeaking, I could have been in an isolation booth.

That's when it started. Slowly, as if someone were whispering in my ear, the sound of wind began to build, even though the air was still. Inexplicably, the sound grew louder and louder for the next ten to fifteen seconds. Finally, I looked around.

There it was!

The funnel of a tornado loomed almost directly behind me, stretching across the sky. At the next house in the complex, I dropped my bike and grabbed onto a basement window ledge as I crouched down. The wind howled as loud as a train blasting past me on a railway platform.

As I turned for one last look, I was surprised that the funnel was swirling in place. It was huge, covering the entire northern sky. Clouds circled in concentric rings from the ground up. It appeared more like a giant screw than a funnel. Debris flew up and down simultaneously, but the swirling clouds were mostly clean, probably because the city didn't have a lot of dust. The most amazing part was red and orange lightning shooting up from the ground, which lit up the clouds' movements, in contrast to the dark sky.

Of course, I had no way of knowing how much damage it was wreaking. I wished I had a camera, because it was like no tornado I had ever—or since—seen in pictures or on TV. To this day, I have no idea how that surreal scene was even possible. If I hadn't been so scared, I probably wouldn't have stopped watching, because it was so oddly beautiful and transfixing.

In the moment, though, I turned my back on the monster, squeezed my eyes shut, and crouched tighter. No sooner did I finish a brief prayer; the noise died down.

Did you hear me, God?

When I turned back around, the beast had vanished.

I knocked on the back door of the house, and the father emerged from the basement with his family peering from behind. My account of the storm enthralled them. Then I used their phone to call my mom, who had been doing laundry in the basement, and had no idea about the tornado. I declined her offer to pick me up, because she hadn't yet learned how to drive, and told her I would be home shortly.

A few minutes after I arrived home, Dad got home, while Mom was recovering from her shock. He had been held up at work, and had just driven through some of the major damage. If he had left on time, there is no telling what might have happened to him.

The two of us decided to delay dinner, and walk to 95th street to investigate. Emergency vehicles arrived as we saw a man, who didn't appear to be breathing, lying in a puddle of water with downed electrical line draped all around. Dad told me to keep my distance, as the wires might be alive.

As we approached 95th street, I was amazed that only the back half of the bus depot remained. The city buses were heaped into a pyramid in the middle of the street, as if the storm had played with them like toy cars. Entire stores were gone. Cars and huge uprooted trees were perched on top of houses—that is, if the roofs hadn't been torn off. Debris was everywhere. Oak Lawn High School was half its size. I'll never forget the bathroom sinks and toilets hanging in midair, suspended by plumbing. We talked as we walked home, but I think we were both stunned.

Later that night, I got a call from my diligent Scoutmaster, Mr. Pozdol, who volunteered our services as Boy Scouts. A state of emergency was declared. Immediate needs were, food and shelter for displaced families, and disaster crews. For the next several days, I collected food from door-to-door for the relief effort. People gave generously, and I made maybe a half dozen trips with a borrowed wagon, to the Oak Lawn First United Methodist Church, where supplies were sorted and stored. Even though I was just a kid, people were depending on me.

The church, serving as a relief center, offered a great buffet for the victims and rescue workers, and I ate alongside police, firefighters, and the National Guard. Most were just grabbing some sandwiches and heading back out. Still, being part of something to help people made a lasting impression on me. The sloppy joes were pretty good too. As a side note, roughly ten years later, the Oak Lawn First United Methodist Church, was the first church Crystal and I joined as a married couple.

The governor declared Oak Lawn to be a disaster area. The relief efforts, on multiple levels, continued for several months. Our troop continued its involvement. For weeks, we helped with the cleanup effort, which included clearing debris from what had been a trailer park. Not one trailer was left standing. (I never shared this with my oldest daughter when she moved into a trailer with her boyfriend.) We found a lot of scrap metal and junk, but occasionally something valuable, such as a wallet or jewelry, to give back to the owners.

There is no doubt that 1967 changed my view of life. The snowstorm, while fun from a kid's point of view, helped me realize that mankind is limited. Our best plans can change quickly. Also, people of authority and science—weather forecasters in particular—aren't always right. The tornado reinforced that lesson, but also demonstrated how fleeting life can be. Thirty-three people lost their lives in the tornado, and another thousand were injured in the tornadoes' extended path, roughly 200 yards wide and 16 miles long, according to the Chicago Tribune article. If it had struck a half hour earlier, another hundred might have been lost in the high school; a half hour later and the bulk of the rush-hour traffic, including my dad, might have been involved.

To this day, I try to enjoy life daily, by looking for the humor and the positives. I learned early that, I'm not in control. God seldom tips his hand. Focus on the good whenever you can, because opportunities may be limited.

Ron, at age thirteen, stands in rubble the day after the tornado of 1967 in Oak Lawn, Illinois.

Surviving High School

Ron

During the 1960s and 70s, urban high schools were overflowing with baby boomers. Harold L. Richards High School was no exception. We were on the two-two system, which referred to different locations for different years of high school. There were three campuses: two for freshmen and sophomores, and a third for juniors and seniors, with a total of four thousand students.

Surprisingly, I never felt like a number or lost. By the end of high school in 1972, I knew the majority of my 969 graduating classmates. Some I just knew by appearance, but many by name and interest. Of course, I related better to members of the many groups I had joined. I was on the college track, so I knew my share of geeks—not that I was one. Band, Boy Scouts, and a little math tutoring don't make me a geek, do they? I hate labels.

Somewhat unusual for the average geek, though, I was into sports. While I never tried out for team sports, I played in pick-up games, wherever and whenever I could find them. I never tried out for the school's football or baseball teams, because of my mother's fear of injury, and my father's attitude of "You need to study more." Also, the team practices didn't sound fun—all work, drills, and pressure. I just wanted to play.

Our school also had a history of losing. While it was still fun going to games with friends, it would have been nice to celebrate a winning record occasionally. I'm sure part of the reason stemmed from our district not yet being integrated. Desegregation busing at Richards started the year after I graduated. I'm glad I missed that. It's not that I'm prejudice; I was ignorant. How could I not be? Oak Lawn was a white community. All I knew of other races is what I heard on the news—race riots, fights, demonstrations. Blacks hurting whites. Whites hurting blacks. The emphasis always seemed to be on skin color. I couldn't relate to any of it.

The first time I heard Martin Luther King Jr. preach in the late sixties on TV, I was more impressed with the way he shouted everything than what he was saying. I thought he was scary, and why was he so mad? The priests in my Catholic church spoke in Latin half the time, and never shouted about anything.

Of course, I didn't know Crystal back then, but I'd heard of her school. Thornridge High School was in our conference, and always made the news for racial problems. Police were stationed there, because blacks and whites fought in the halls. Students were frisked for weapons. However, they were basketball champions, so I had mixed feelings about a multi-race school.

Girls weren't a big part of my life—again, mainly out of ignorance. Sophomore year, I asked out a cute greaser. You know, one of those long-haired beauties who hung out with the leather jackets, smoking just off of school property. She called me a fem. When I found out she meant I was too feminine, that did it for girls.

Years later, I discovered that other girls had noticed me, and thought I was smart and funny. They said they would have dated me. It's probably better the way it was. I would have been like a dog chasing a car; I wouldn't have known what to do if I caught one.

I did have some moves, though. I gave a few free tennis and skiing lessons. I considered myself a good instructor. Of course, in the back of my mind, I hoped the grateful girl would ask me to make out behind a tree. Why did that never work?

I also showed off my tree-climbing skills to girls. In high school and even college, I would run up a tree trunk to the lowest branch, pull myself up, and ascend rapidly. It was a conversation starter, but little more. While I tried to impress them with athleticism, I may just have instead been advertising my immaturity. Or maybe they thought I was demonstrating that, at least one of us would survive if we were attacked by a bear. Needless to say, outside of a few monkey references, not a great move.

While I wasn't smart with the ladies, my class rank was an acceptable 162 out of 969, and I got a composite 23 on the ACT. Back then that put me in the top 20% of college freshmen. While no genius, I was college bound.

Crystal

I studied hard and strived for straight A's at Thornridge High School in Dolton, about fifteen miles from where Ron lived in Oak Lawn. My dad joked that I ruined the curve on tests for the other students.

Thornridge was sometimes a hostile environment, so I stayed under the radar. I had a variety of friends, dated occasionally, and avoided trouble. My black friends and I helped each other be safe when fights broke out in the hallways. My main extracurricular activities were the debate team, the speech team, and the literary magazine.

During my junior and senior years, I was an editor and writer for *The Talisman* magazine, which won big awards in the statewide contests. This influenced me to major in English in college, and focus on literature and creative writing.

To this day, I still complain about how non-sport activities, such as debating, public speaking, and writing, are ignored by the media, students, and well, just about everyone. One word of advice that Ron gives: If you marry a debater, don't be surprised if you lose some arguments.

My diligence paid off with my class rank of 11, out of 660 Seniors, and high standardized testing scores. A number of good schools offered me four-year scholarships. However, I decided to attend Thornton Community College for my first two years, because I wasn't ready to leave home. I got along well with my family, and was involved in our church and the community. Plus, my mom had some health issues, and frequently required help. When I wasn't studying, I helped clean the house, did laundry, made meals, and cared for my younger sister.

At Thornton Community College, I wrote for the newspaper and literary magazine, and I won first place in a community writing contest. For my last two years, I transferred to Bradley University for its great English department, and was an editor and writer for the school's literary magazine.

Bradley University

Ron

After falling in love with Peoria, Illinois, I never doubted I would choose Bradley University. My first view of the city along the Illinois River sold me on it. As we rounded the bend on Interstate 74, Peoria reminded me of a dwarf Chicago, with the downtown over the suspension bridge. The people weren't as uptight, though.

A state park, and a steam-powered paddleboat graced the city, along with a brand-new mall. Mansions lined a winding road called High Street, overlooking the river. During the 1920s and 1930s, Al Capone and other Chicago gangsters blew off steam in them. Thank God, it was the seventies.

The hilly, residential, and forested areas close to the downtown instantly made me feel comfortable. Scouting had given me a strong appreciation for nature. The school was up a hill on Main Street, about a mile from downtown. It was a walk I took many times.

The campus was just the right size, with about four thousand students. The history of some of the buildings was obvious. Ivy-shrouded buildings abounded. As a chemistry major, I spent a lot of time in Olin Hall, which was a brand-new showpiece in the middle of campus. It had the familiar chemical smell, that I had grown to love from my dad's lab. Little did I know that, learning about where that smell came from would be a tedious, extremely painful process. There was a reason why, the sixty chemistry majors in my freshmen class dwindled to fourteen by the time I graduated.

In the spring of 1972, the professors seemed great and friendly. Students threw Frisbees and baseballs on campus, and read under trees. A block off campus, was Laura Bradley Park. During my Bradley years I frequently studied, or went for a run, and played softball or tennis there. The gently hilly, wooded area gave me a sense of peace.

I was impressed that the university had a real computer. In fact, the IBM System/360 had its own building. The many components of the mainframe sprawled throughout the first floor, with a minimum of two full-time operators around the clock. The second floor was full of keypunch machines. I later found the whole process to be mental torture.

One of my first projects was to calculate a salesman's commission, which I could figure out in my head in a matter of minutes. However, with me doing the programming, the process took closer to three weeks. That's how long, with my typing skills, it took to generate an accurate stack of key punch cards about an inch thick.

When I ran my first stack, it took about twenty-four hours to get it back. I was excited to see the results, but the program was prematurely terminated due to "operator request." One of the world's first computer geeks had dissed my program for no apparent reason. Two days later, my professor scribbled red marks all over my beautiful program. After surviving that class, I swore I would never have anything to do with a computer again… Who knew?

The summer before my freshman year, I attended a mandatory orientation session. After settling into a dorm room for the first time, after a full day of orientation, I received an invitation to a fraternity mixer. I had no clue. What was a fraternity? A mixer sounded like party, though, so I was in.

At the fraternity house, members passed out beers to anyone willing. I was amazed nobody cared that we were drinking. I threw back four beers so quickly, that I barely heard them talking about rush and fraternity life. I stumbled outside to throw up.

As I walked back to the dorm, the world was shifting in a mysterious pattern—counterclockwise, I think. I noticed a man following me—my height, neatly groomed, muscular, with a mustache and some stubble. Was I about to get a lecture about the evils of barfing on campus? My parents would kill me, or even worse, try to homeschool me through college.

Thank goodness, the man turned out to be a fellow freshman named Wayne, who asked me to be his roommate. We made a good pair, but Wayne became one of the many students who lasted only a year. I struggled through freshman year with little better than a C average. Nobody told me college would be hard! OK everybody told me, but I chose not to listen.

My first month led me to the core group in my life for the next four years: Corky, Carol, Larry, Perry, and Rose. We still stay loosely in touch, like a group of soldiers who fought a war together, if only through Christmas cards. We had a similar mission: to graduate. We shared struggles, pain, joy, play, and support.

Rose was a diminutive nursing student from southern Illinois. She had a slight, but strong build with long, silky brown hair. In case you haven't guessed, I had a thing for her. However, we were never more than good friends.

Rose and her freshman roommate, Debbie, made me their pet project. While I tried to project a man-of-the-world image, they saw through it to my inexperience with women. Although Rose loved teasing me, she explained things clinically like a nurse, such as menstruation. I had paid no attention during the lecture in seventh grade.

One day, Debbie dragged me into the art building with a big smile. As an art major, she had full access. She told me to follow her into the classroom, and focus on the students' sketches. To my great surprise and delight, it was a nude study, with a woman posing somewhat provocatively, and staring aimlessly at the ceiling.

While this was my first naked lady, it was hardly my last. Streaking was big in the seventies. One day, the local news reported that, Bradley's fraternities were organizing one for that evening. Sure enough, I watched all the proud guys and coeds bounce by at 10 that night. The next day, we watched the news, and cheered as students we knew were shown from non-revealing angles.

Most of my dating experiences at school were rather innocent. I simply enjoyed women's company, and occasional kissing. I wanted to understand women. I found most guys to be predictable… women, not so much. Today, after forty-plus years of marriage and three daughters, I still don't understand much. However, I'm fairly certain that I'm not alone. Most men and even many women—if they are honest—don't understand women either.

I found dating to be a great distraction from the constant pressure of studying. Rose encouraged me to ask out women. Once I conquered my shyness, I realized they *might* say yes if I asked.

I also discovered that women, even before the age of social networking, used a social network to spread information, especially about guys. After I started dating Crystal, she divulged that she had asked three women about me, and got roughly the same report—a nice, intelligent, humorous, and safe guy. The only part I had any problem with, was being known as safe. I know they meant well, but in my mind, it sounded somewhat as if I had been neutered.

Crystal was a year behind me and was a driven student. I don't think she ever got a B until she got to Bradley, ironically in chemistry. While my parents were advising me to study more, hers were encouraging her to have more fun. I guess that's why we were so well suited.

A.P.O.

Ron

In the freshmen men's dorm, we did everything from riding bikes down the stairs to launching bottle rockets down the hall, and watching the resident advisor run down the stairs to chase the seemingly invisible culprit. He never caught on. We were at the other end of the hall watching him go where he heard the explosion.

That fall, we all went through fraternity rush, and I was the only who wasn't asked to pledge in a Fraternity. I still have no idea why I was snubbed, but I am truly grateful. Sometimes I think God saves me from myself. I had a great time my first two years as a GDI, or gosh darn independent (cleaned up slightly).

By the time Junior year rolled around, I was living in a rooming house just off campus, my grades were off the critical list, and to my surprise, I was even starting to understand chemistry. One day in the gym, my friend Larry roped me into refereeing a basketball game for his service fraternity, called Alpha Phi Omega (APO). The next day, he talked to me about their football team.

It wasn't long before I realized this was no ordinary fraternity. They weren't serious about winning. They had maybe three or four athletes, but the rest were just there to have fun. Soon, I was kicking, punting, returning kickoffs and punts, catching passes—my favorite things. Larry also invited me to a party. They didn't have a house like other frats, but they had parties at least every other weekend, at one student's apartment or another.

When he knew he had hooked me, he gave me the whole story. Apparently, APO stemmed from the Boy Scouts and was based on leadership, friendship, and service. This was an organization for guys who wanted to not only have fun, but also help others. They had connections to the community and national organizations, such as the Red Cross, Salvation Army, and the American Cancer Society. Almost every Saturday morning, they worked on a project to help the school, or a charitable organization achieve a goal.

If Larry had led with that, he probably would have lost me. My Saturday mornings were sacred for sleeping late and watching cartoons. He also failed to mention that he was in charge of recruiting, and had a vested interest. As a former Scout, however, I knew the service projects wouldn't kill me. One final selling point: The organization had roughly twice the number of little sisters as brothers. Where else could you find that ratio? Certainly not in the chemistry department.

I joined, and President Tommy got his swat on my butt with a paddle. In my two years with APO, I served as the athletic director and vice president. I gained good leadership experience, while helping people and having fun. Service included helping prepare the local Boy Scout camp in the spring, painting buildings, aluminum can and paper drives, manning checkpoints for bike-a-thons, and tearing down buildings. I enjoyed the physical activities, which put me in a good state of mind for study. During football and basketball seasons, we usually had a game in the afternoon, and a party at night. Obviously,

Saturday wasn't the best study day, but I still felt a sense of accomplishment.

We were making the community and college administration happy, unlike some other organizations. To reward us, the Dean asked us to provide security and ushers for concerts. I got paid five dollars per event, could bring a date, and got to watch the concert for free. The concerts were held on campus at the Robertson Memorial Field House, named after a former coach. Built in 1949 out of two World War II air plane hangars, it hosted the university's basketball games, and various major events in Peoria. Even President Gerald Ford visited in 1975 to defend his budget.

While I hadn't met Crystal yet, this was one of the first events on campus that she attended. She insists that, she was thrilled to touch the President's hand while he was shaking hands as he passed by.

I got to see some excellent concerts, including The Carpenters, Johnny Cash, and Harry Chapin. The last concert I worked was Sly and the Family Stone. I thought this would be a great chance to broaden my musical horizons. I knew I would be part of a minority, but wasn't worried. For the most part, racial tension which, were high a few years earlier, had died down at Bradley by the mid-seventies. This was all about the music.

A huge line formed for the Sly concert. When people started kicking the side doors, I told the head of security. After everyone was seated, I had to sit in the top row because the place was packed. People became restless when the concert didn't start on time, shouting, stomping their feet, and passing brown bags and special cigarettes. I'd never seen such a widespread smoke-a-thon.

After forty-five minutes, I left because I was dizzy from the height, and second-hand smoke. Besides, I needed to study for a test. As I walked outside, I noticed that panels were missing in the doors that had been kicked. At some point, I think it might have become a free concert.

I know I made the right decision. The next couple of days, the news reported on the concert, which started two hours late, and involved the police being called in to the overcrowded stadium, for crowd control.

Thankfully, there was more harmony in my living quarters, which I called the United Nations Boarding House. The owner, Mr. Magnusson, was a seventy-year-old Christian Scientist, who won a gold medal as an Olympic walker in 1932. The boarders were a variety of ethnicities. A student from Hawaii let me borrow his 1972 Dodge Super Bee car. One of the two Vietnamese students was a computer major; and I probably wouldn't have gotten through computer science without his help. A Polish scientist worked with me at the Department of Agriculture labs in town. And I ate a beef heart sandwich with two Arab students named Mohammad and Ali (yes real names).

Our fraternity used to practice basketball on Sunday afternoons at an outdated gym facility from 1908, called Hewitt Hall. One little problem: The Gothic-styled, ivy-covered, limestone building had two sides. One side had open gym, and was generally crowded with guys. The other was the women's gym, which was closed on weekends. As APO's athletic director, I knew we needed all of the practice we could get. I figured out a way to work-around the restrictions.

On Friday afternoons, I would unlatch a second-floor window in the women's gym. Then on Sunday, when no one was watching, I would climb up the drainpipe and through the unlatched window. Then I moseyed downstairs to open the door for our practice. No one ever caught us. One day, however, a security person came up and said to me, I thought this building was supposed to be closed on Sundays. He asked me to lock up when we were done, and I gave him my word. And I kept my word.

One of my APO friends felt like a true brother to me. Dominic, was a second-generation American of Italian descent. We talked like brothers, acted like brothers, and even argued like brothers. In fact, people asked if we were related. Even after college, we stayed close. He was the best man at our wedding, and became very close to Crystal also. She wrote, emailed, and talked to him on the phone more than I did.

To my three girls, he was Uncle Dom. He played with them, sent them presents, and made them laugh. He was a ray of sunshine in all of our lives. We last saw him on Labor Day of 2009, before he tragically died of a massive heart attack at the age fifty-four.

Dom, if you're somehow reading this, we miss you.

Meeting Crystal

Ron

I didn't go to college thinking I would find a mate. However, I always knew that I would one day have a wife and, hopefully, kids. Because of that probability, and my faith, I started adding a couple of things to my prayers. First, I started praying for the woman to whom God would lead me. I prayed that she was doing well, and was well suited for me (even if I had no idea what that meant). My second prayer was that, God make it obvious for me. It should be like hitting me on the head with a rolled-up newspaper. Several years later I found out that, Crystal had been praying a similar prayer for me.

While I had no clue when I would meet the right girl, Crystal was determined to stick to her plan. First, she would finish college, with the best GPA possible. Next, she would move to Oregon to become a great writer. She had heard that a lot of artistic types were in Oregon. She would fit in. Then, she would marry and start her family. In that scenario, to me, the guy seemed like a sort of afterthought. God, apparently knew better. Someday, however, we hope to take a trip to Oregon. I went with my parents as a youth. It's where I shot my first gun, and milked my first goat. It's a beautiful state.

I didn't really get my second prayer answered. Figuring out girls, and God's Will, have rarely been obvious to me. By the time I was a college senior, I had a fair amount of dating experience, and lots of different types of relationships with women. Outside of dating, I had everything from study partners, to tennis partners, to fellow shutter bugs (photographers). There was even one girl with whom, I used to take afternoon naps. It was just convenient. We were both between classes. A nap was good after lunch, and I didn't have to hike to my room off campus. She had a boyfriend at another school, but insisted that I had the best shoulder to sleep on. I was never sure if a guy having a soft shoulder was a good thing.

One day, our nap caused me a problem. While I rested well, I could seldom fall asleep in the afternoon. One day, however, I did. I woke up to find I was a half hour late for my Organic Qualitative Analysis lab. When I rushed into my lab, my lab partner, and future roommate, George was still there. He had not given up on me, but had started some homework on one of the lab benches. I apologized and explained my dilemma. He was fascinated, and asked me to share some of my worldly wisdom on women. While a good example of the blind leading the blind, unfortunately, this became the predominate topic of conversation that afternoon. We probably should have paid a little more attention to properly interpreting our instructions.

We had an idea about the identity of the unknown compound. In order to prove it, we needed to make a derivative. As we began, one of the professors brought a group of freshmen students into our lab, to take a test. Sitting at the benches, they could be spread apart properly to eliminate temptation.

We were still quietly discussing our topic of the day when we reached the part of the procedure which, was marked in quotes, 'A vigorous reaction will occur.' If we had been focusing, we probably could have anticipated what happened next. As we added one compound to the other, the mixture started boiling rapidly. We stopped the addition, and turned off the flame. This only seemed to make it mad. A fume of dense white smoke was now filling the hood. That particular hood never seemed to work very well. Soon the beaker was sputtering, and then began jumping up and down. The smoke was now pouring into the lab. We were still trying to control the reaction when one of the professors came in, and rescued the freshmen, who had started to cough and wheeze from the smoke. The dense white smoke had now covered the entire ceiling of the lab. When I say cover, I mean, you could barely see the ceiling.

Another professor came in and yelled, 'Who is pumping hydrochloric acid into my instruments?' He stopped only long enough to give us a dirty look, and disappeared again. We finally threw a couple of handfuls of ice on the mess, and left the room coughing and gagging. To this day, it still bothers me a little, that, while the precious Freshmen were quickly saved, us poor Jr. Chemists were left by two professors to die. By the time we re-entered the lab, my lab partner had explained, in great detail, the reaction which had occurred, and all the noxious gasses generated. George was even higher on the geek scale than I. The lab experiment that should have taken about three hours, wound up taking about six. It was at that point that I realized, even the topic of girls, could cause problems.

Back on the subject of girls, there were several girls whom I dated, I thought might make good mates for me. Those relationships, however, always got to a certain point, and for one reason or another, ended.

My senior year was Crystal's first year at Bradley. While she was quite home sick for a while, her experience was similar to mine, in finding friends right away. She got along great with her roommate, Debra, and had several close friends on her floor. A girl named Puddin was my favorite. She liked running around the floor in her night gown. Of course, I only liked her for her personality. Crystal didn't join a sorority, but after meeting my friend Larry Rose, when he was promoting Alpha Phi Omega, became a little sister pledge. She had grown up helping people with her family through the church, and in the community, and liked the goals of APO: leadership, friendship and service.

She first noticed me at the APO square dance and hay ride. I had a date from outside of APO. Crystal didn't talk to me, but was impressed with my manners and attentiveness (her words not mine). My parents had raised me to be a gentleman.

The event where I finally met Crystal was a sister organized event. It was a 1950's party. Just like the show "Happy Days" or the play "West Side Story".

Neither Dominic nor I knew much about dressing for the 50's. So, we went in the James Dean/Sha Na Na direction. We dressed in blue jeans, tee shirts, and hair slicked back with enough oil to lube a sedan. I even borrowed a pack of cigarettes to roll under my shirt sleeve. We found a couple of ropes to use as belts, and Dom had a chain over his shoulder. We looked bad.

When we got to the party, we were greeted at the door by a couple of the sisters. They had gone all out. The place was decorated like a school gym before a sock hop.

There were school banners and pompoms on the wall; the girls were in skirts, blouses and bobby socks. There were even a few lettermen's jackets. "Rock Around the Clock" was already blasting. Most brothers had the same idea we did, with the exception of a few, who didn't bother to dress up. The girls were impressed with our costume efforts, and gave us the 'I'm scared tough guy' look (if there is such a thing).

Crystal was the last of the greeters, standing a little more in the room than the rest. I know it's not polite to stare, but I couldn't help it. I felt as if I had never seen legs before. First of all, you didn't see many girls' legs around campus, as blue jeans or slacks were standard dress. But her long lanky legs were perfect. I started looking around for the rest of the Rockettes. Alas, she was alone. She directed me to the refreshment table in the kitchen and the garbage can punch. Garbage can punch can be a special treat, if properly prepared. First, you buy a new garbage can, and rinse it thoroughly. Previous attempts to clean a used garbage can had failed miserably. Next, as each participant comes in, they add a pint of their favorite alcohol. Some screening is required. Certain flavors like Cream de Menthe could prove fatal to the punch. Finally, punch ingredients like Hawaiian punch, lemonade, and 7-up were added. I felt a certain responsibility to assure its quality. As the Frat's only Chemistry major, I could make the critical calculations. Many years of experimentation had gone into a pursuit of the perfect punch. While perfection of flavor could never be agreed upon, some facts had been established. The most critical is that, you should maintain your punch at a moderate level of alcohol. I figured between five and eight percent (you start a little high to allow for melting ice). This way you could drink it much the same as you would beer. Also, if you get to much less than four percent it would become harder to achieve the desired effect. If you go much over eight percent, many of the girls would stop drinking, and again you would fail to achieve the desired effect. However, just to be nice, and for possible use as diluents, soft drinks were also made available for those not wishing to partake in the punch ritual.

At any rate, once I had taken all the empty bottles and back calculated the proper dilution ratio, I adjusted the punch, and talked to a few brothers, who joined me in admiring my craftsmanship. Several cups of admired craftsmanship later, I went back into the living room, where everyone was standing around, talking with the music blaring. Crystal was standing in the corner, looking kind of shy, and obviously checking out all of the interesting characters. I walked right up to her, bolstered slightly by artificial courage, and started to talk to her. At first, she looked at me kind of strangely. I had forgotten about my costume. While I had never really been attracted to a particular type of girl, blonde hair and blue eyes worked. At five seven, this skinny girl was almost as tall as me; and it was easy to talk to her. I proudly offered her some punch, and asked her if she would dance with me. We might have been the first to dance that night, but others soon joined. We both knew just enough jitter bug to get by. When she looked too tired to continue, we sat down on the couch, and continued our conversation. I never used a line with girls. I don't think I could have used one and kept a straight face. I did, however, have a huge repertoire of interests. I knew a little bit about a variety of subjects. When she told me, she was an English major, I said something about liking literature. She was immediately skeptical. If her face could speak, it would have said, "Yeah right!" Apparently, she had met guys in the past that actually lied to her; hard to believe, right? Little did she know that, I was only exaggerating for effect. That's different, isn't it? Rather than be tortured by more writing and grammar classes, I had actually struggled through elective courses in English and American Literature in High School. I knew enough to throw around some names and titles. When she tried to pin down my favorite, without much hesitation I said Thoreau. This wasn't a total lie. I loved the concepts from *Walden Pond.* Living a simple life in the woods by a lake sounded great. What I failed to mention was that I found the verbiage difficult to understand, and reading more than a page at a time was a sure cure for the insomnia from which, I had never suffered. A more honest answer would have been Poe or even Dickens. Both are totally respectable authors, but didn't sound as classy. At least I could half way understand Thoreau, if I had gone with Shakespeare or, worse yet Milton, I would have given it away. When forced to watch Romeo and Juliet in high school, I actually preferred a similar plot done in the 70's sitcom "Three's Company". It wasn't so overdone, or sad.

At any rate, our conversation was going well, except for the fact that another girl kept jumping into my lap. She obviously had enjoyed the punch, and needed to show her appreciation. I promised the lap jumper that, I would save a dance for her, which seemed to appease her. I asked Crystal if she would take a walk with me. She agreed. Up until that point she had been fairly quiet. Once outside she admitted to being a little tired after a rough week. She also confided in me that, she was supposed to meet one of my fraternity brothers at the party. He had stood her up. She didn't seem to trust me very much either. About half way around the block we stopped on some church steps. She stopped talking, looked me in the eyes, and I leaned toward her. The next words are what every guy can't wait to hear. "What are you doing???"

I told her, "I thought you wanted me to kiss you."

I honestly did think that! I then tried to pretend nothing had happened, and suggested we return to the party. We finished our walk, and I thanked her for the dance and walk. I spent a little more time at the party, drinking, talking to others, and a little more dancing (including the lap jumper girl), and I headed home.

Sometime later, Crystal told me two things about that first encounter. First was that, when she first saw me, slicked hair and all, a small voice in her head said "this is the one". That confused her, since she was in no way attracted to what she saw. I do believe in intuition, and that, prayers to God work. Secondly was that, when she went back to the dorm, she ranted for a while to her roommate about guys. First, she griped about being stood up. Then about the guy who said he liked literature, and tried to steal a kiss. Without ever meeting me, Debra was immediately on my side. She said, maybe I was telling the truth. Also, here Crystal was all made up, with a cute top and that poodle skirt (I don't remember there being a poodle above her legs). He couldn't help himself. I think I also had scored a major point with Debra, by not being named Steve. At the time Crystal had been seeing four boys named Steve. The "you got a call from Steve" bit had gotten old. For clarification, they called them tall Steve; short Steve, fraternity Steve and political Steve (who was involved with Bradley's student government).

The Dance

Ron

After that day, things quieted down a little between Crystal and me. While I was friendly, and talked to her at parties and work projects, I kept a little distance. I think I was still a little embarrassed about trying to kiss her. Besides, I wasn't that interested in her, and was dating other girls whom I had known longer. Then came our fraternity's semi-formal dance. As was my nature, I procrastinated. I waited until the week of the dance to start asking girls. I wasn't worried. The year before I had gone by myself and had a great time. Just like most APO parties, a lot of girls showed up without dates. This year, I really wanted to take a date. I asked six girls. Most already had dates, or were going home. I was just about out of options and ready to give up. It was only a couple days until formal when I decided to make one more call. Crystal was already getting grief from her friend Amy, about none of the Steves coming through. To my surprise, Crystal seemed honestly glad that I called, and gratefully accepted. We would double with Amy and Doug.

Then there was the restaurant debate. Neither Doug nor I had an abundant revenue stream. We agreed to either take the girls to one of the less expensive options (Chinese restaurant or pizza/Italian place) or go Dutch, to a nice place. Crystal was OK either way. One thing

I've always liked about her is that, she is easy to please. She told me that, eating out when she was young usually meant that, her dad would pick up White Castle burgers, on his way home. Amy, however, wasn't about to dress up to go to a Chinese restaurant. The girls decided on a nice steak restaurant, and would pay for their own dinners. As much as I hate to admit it, Amy was right. That was better.

I was impressed with how nice we all looked that night. I was wearing my one and only suit, and Crystal looked especially nice in her evening dress. I had made reservations for dinner. That was another first for me. Everything was perfect at dinner. The restaurant was great. We entered through an old railroad car. The theme was all about the railroad. From lanterns to the dark, wood paneled walls with train pictures, you could picture a dining car. There were candles and real table cloths. The food was great too. Even Amy couldn't complain.

On our way to the country club, which APO had reserved for the dance, I almost threw Amy out of the car. I had known Amy for quite some time. While I liked her, I never had to wonder what was on her mind; she told me. After about the fifth comment about my driving, I pulled over and stopped the car. I told her; maybe if I was such a bad driver, she would be safer walking. She declined my invitation, and was much quieter (not her natural state) after that. I actually think my thoughtful gesture impressed Crystal.

When we got to the dance, the music was already blaring. My first impression was how really nice and grown up everyone appeared that night. When you are used to seeing people in blue jeans, and all at once they are in suits and dresses, you take notice. Guys were clean shaven and girls had make-up on. I never attended a prom, but think the shock factor must have been similar. The beer was flowing freely, and the dancing had begun. While we looked good, our taste in music hadn't changed. Our regular party music included songs like "Blueberry Hill" and "Saturday Night's Alright". The big song that year was a novelty, the Chuck Berry classic "My Ding-A-Ling", to which we all sang along. I could tell Crystal was enjoying herself. After dancing for a while, we went outside and talked. It was cold but we kept close, which was nice. Together, we looked over the dark golf course, in the moon light. It was very romantic. After a while we returned and danced a little more. We then sat on the couch. Crystal was obviously tired. To my surprise, she actually fell asleep on the couch. I could have been insulted, but instead was a little impressed. I thought, she must be really comfortable with me to fall asleep on our date. I spent the next hour or two dancing with some of the girls, who came without dates. It was a win win scenario.

Eventually, Amy came up to me, and suggested that, I scoop up my date (those might have been her exact words) so we could hit the road. We made it home without incident. I pulled up to her dorm; Crystal said good night, jumped out and walked quickly into the building. I thought it was cute that she was so shy. It never occurred to me, that she didn't really know me that well, and was uneasy. I knew that, I would never do anything against a girl's wishes, but a girl wouldn't automatically know that. At any rate, I thought the date was a rousing success, and Crystal was now officially on my radar.

Crystal

I remember that first date very well. It was on November 15, 1975. Our mutual friend, Amy, who lived on my floor, helped to set it up. I was very excited about the date, because I hadn't gone to Prom, or any of the high school dances. None of my high school boyfriends took me. I wore a beautiful long dress, with long sleeves and a full skirt. The fabric had a soft, cream background with red orange roses, which was perfect for a fall dance. My mom had made the dress for me to stand up with my close friend, Laura, at her wedding in September. It was very elegant.

Ron wore a nice suit. We ate at a restaurant that had been converted from railroad cars, and the depot where we ate. The meal included steak, baked potatoes and salad. Ron had excellent manners, was very attentive to me the whole time, and prayed before we started eating. The dance was held at a very nice country club in a rural area. There was a fireplace, nice couches and furniture to rest on. I had been dealing with tonsillitis for several years and especially that fall. It had been a long day. I worked in downtown Peoria, for a law firm every Saturday from 8 a.m. to noon. After dancing several dances, I rested on the couch, while he danced with other little sisters in our group.

To me, the entire date was like a dream. It was as if I had been waiting for a date like that my whole life, and Ron was the best part of it. He had beautiful brown eyes with long lashes, a great smile, and a wonderful sense of humor. I felt very safe and happy being with him. I didn't, however, let him walk me back to my dorm room, but like Cinderella at midnight, I jumped out of the car and ran. The next day was Sunday. He came over wearing gym shorts, bouncing a basketball. My roommate, Debra, let him into my room where I was studying. He talked to me and I backed up against the wall, and he gave me the goodnight kiss I didn't let him give me the night before. It was some kiss. Also, he asked me out again. He would call me on Tuesday night to ask me out for Saturday night, like a true gentleman. I appreciated that. The girls in the dorm couldn't believe it. Most of their dates called a few hours before taking them out.

We talked a great deal on our dates, covering many subjects including family, religion, places we wanted to go, and more. It seemed to me that he was too good to be true. I had been hurt before by dishonest people. So, I decided to analyze his handwriting, using a book I took out of the library. Debra thought I was crazy. She liked Ron immediately after meeting him, and thought we were a great couple. She trusted him. The analysis came out fine. I actually thought that it would.

Ron

Today, so many years later, I know that I have come down from that pedestal more than a few times. What I find so wonderful, and should be obvious to anyone reading, Crystal still remembers that day in such vivid detail. Even these days, on occasion, and I can see it in her eyes, when I do or say something that helps her remember. Also, while at the time I didn't see it, and happily ever after would be a stretch, she is still my Cinderella.

Courtship

Ron

While, when we met, Crystal believed God may have told her I was, "the one", my decision-making process wasn't nearly so clear cut. After our first date at the APO semi-formal dance, I still dated around. In fact, I took Rose, as my date, to the wedding of my friend, Keith. He had dated a cute, quiet woman named Hope before moving onto his future wife, Faith. While I noticed a pattern emerging, he never got past Faith, and proposed to her his Senior year. Larry was his best man, and I was a groomsman. This was another sign that I wasn't a kid anymore. This was my first wedding, and I was a groomsman, tux and everything.

I barely noticed Crystal at the reception, but was preoccupied with being a good host for Rose, and everything going on. She, however, saw me and was offended that, I appeared to ignore her. Like most guys, I was oblivious to her pain. Near the end of the event, our mutual friend, Amy, and Rose pointed Crystal out to me. Amy was never subtle, of course. I believe she threatened to hit me on the nose with something. I immediately asked Crystal to dance and apologized for my unintended snub. I could see she was happy with my attention. We talked for a while before I took Rose home.

The next day, I showed up at her dorm room and talked her into taking a study break. We walked and talked for a couple of hours, until she heard her books calling. After that day, we spent more and more time together.

I soon noticed we were good for each other. I infused her life with fun, and she taught me better study habits. We helped each other whenever possible. She typed my papers, and I gave her and her friends rides when they needed a lift.

One day, she had to get a tetanus shot after scraping her knees during a fall in a campus parking lot. The side effects knocked her off her feet with body aches, chills, and a low-grade fever. Her room resembled a dreary cave, so I drove her to my place and tucked her into my bed. I tried to make her as comfortable as possible, and helped her stay hydrated.

It was just my luck that Mr. Magnusson picked that afternoon to show a room to a couple of potential female tenants. He knocked on the door and joked,

"Hey, Ron, I've got a couple of girls for you."

When I opened the door, he saw Crystal on my bed and said,

"Oh, I see you've already got one." Next door, Dominic started laughing uncontrollably. That was the end of the girls' tour.

Many things impressed me about Crystal. She could talk about anything, loved to learn, and was easy to please. If I bought her an ice-cream cone or a cookie, she squealed with excitement. We took leisurely walks in the park or drives in the country. She appreciated when I cooked for her or packed a lunch.

Crystal was never athletic, but would try new things with me, such as tennis and jogging. One day, we even went rock climbing, and I made her pose in precarious positions nearly a hundred feet over the Illinois River. She couldn't wait to show her skeptical family. Unfortunately, I later discovered that I had never put film in the camera. To this day, she hasn't forgiven me for that one, although we've relegated it to a humorous anecdote. We have many of those. In fact, I think it's one of the keys to our successful marriage. You need those kinds of stories and the ability to laugh at yourself. It builds a bond that helps you through the tough times.

One of our special rituals was watching the sunset from the dorm roof. Bradley is on a hill, and is known for its beautiful sunsets. Many students took a break in the red and golden twilight for some peace. Crystal and I would hold hands and kiss—if no one was looking.

No matter where we have lived throughout our marriage, we've enjoyed sunsets and walks together. These moments in nature continue to connect us. Courtship isn't supposed to end with marriage. After forty plus years, we are still dating, and setting an example for our children and grandchildren.

I think it makes God happy when his children are good to each other. I am never happier than when I've done something that makes Crystal happy. I know she feels the same way. It's no longer about everything that makes us individually happy. With all the selfishness in today's society today, I think it is harder to be happily married.

Crystal

While we were dating at Bradley, I was honored when the English Department asked me to read my poetry during the Family Weekend festivities. My parents couldn't come, but Ron brought his parents.

Under the white tent, my hands were sweating, and I was almost shaking. I was afraid I was going to trip on the way to the podium, or drop my papers. Why had I agreed to do this?

While I was reading my first poem, the hourly bells sounded off, so I had to pause. I calmed down as I continued, though, and Ron really touched me by the way he looked at me. He was so proud of me, which meant everything to me. It reinforced our connection and solidified us as a couple.

The fall term of my senior year was difficult and overwhelming. Plus, I was so out of cash that, I read a textbook in the bookstore every other day, and checked out the few assigned books that were sometimes available in the library. I worked there part time, so I would know when the books were available. Ron was taking a few classes that fall, after his Senior year, in order to graduate. He was not under the stress I was experiencing.

One day when Ron asked me to type a paper on deadline, I exploded. He left, so I assumed he was mad at me. However, I later found my friends chatting about a real pumpkin sitting in front of my door. Ron had cut out the stem and replaced it with a beautiful pink rose. I was relieved he wasn't angry with me. His artistic gift let me know that he loved me, and understood that I was under a lot of pressure. I was lucky to have the most thoughtful boyfriend on campus.

Today, Ron still buys me flowers or sweet treats to surprise me, and he always remembers our anniversary, Mother's Day, and my birthday. But the real test of love is saying we love each other every day, along with smiles, hugs, and kisses. We also laugh every day, and often engage in meaningful discussions.

I grew up with loving parents, who were crazy about each other and us. I always wanted to go home from college for their hugs, and words of encouragement and concern. Of course, Ron and I get angry, and struggle to communicate sometimes, but our strong love and faith in each other guide us through.

"Will You Marry Me?"

Ron

After my Senior year, I still had a couple more classes to complete for my degree in the fall of 1976. By this time Crystal and I were very serious, and talked about marriage frequently. We got engaged that fall, and then again six months later in the winter of 1977. That's right, twice.

I proposed the first time during a beautiful walk in Laura Bradley Park, not far from the Bradley Campus. I thought I had all the bases covered. We had been talking about the type of marriage we wanted. Unbeknownst to her, I had already asked and received her father's blessing for her hand. I've always been a little old-fashioned.

It was a cool fall afternoon. We wore light jackets. On our way down the hill, she told me—at my prompting—that it would be great to marry me. Finally, we arrived at the preordained spot: a boulder in a small clearing beside a babbling brook. I had scouted the area privately, earlier. I don't think I ever brought Crystal there before. I hoisted her onto the rock and crouched to one knee. I opened the precious little box, and offered the elegant white gold diamond ring. It was a small, but certified perfect stone, with other smaller stones around it. I told her how much I loved her, and asked her to marry me.

She smiled, but looked surprised. After a moment, she said yes. On the way back she told me that I really surprised her. The ring really suited her, because it was delicate like her.

A few days later, however, she told me she wasn't ready, and handed me the ring. It just wasn't time yet. Apparently, being engaged puts extra pressure on women, and she was too focused on school. Welcome to the confusing way women think! While we had frequently talked about marital decisions (where to live, kids, etc.), to Crystal, at that time, it was scarier to be engaged than married. I was frustrated and confused, but I still loved her, and she still loved me.

After I graduated in January 1977, while she was on break from Bradley, I took her on a date at Senese's Winery Family Restaurant in Oak Lawn, Illinois. For the second time, I handed her my ring, this time across the table without kneeling. I told her this was her last chance. I was only half joking and she knew it. That time, she accepted without reservation, and has worn my ring ever since. While I don't totally understand why Crystal didn't want to be engaged in the Fall of 1976, she made it clear she wanted to marry me. She told me that when girls get engaged everyone asks them questions about the wedding and plans, and she was too overwhelmed with college to deal with the stress. I think, with only one semester left at Bradley, she was able to deal with our being engaged. She and her mom started to make plans, and really worked on them after she graduated in the spring of 1977.

Our engagement zipped by in little more than a year. Our similar ideologies made it easier to work through conflicts. We were truly in love, and believed God would bless our marriage.

At one point, Crystal's sister Jeannette threatened to hit Crystal, if she didn't stop quoting me during their conversations. Apparently, I was very wise back then. Crystal still considers me fairly intelligent, but my indisputable authority diminished shortly after our wedding.

Picking a wedding date was easy. After Crystal graduated, she began saving for our wedding. We naturally agreed she could make most of the decisions, including the month. She picked April 1978, which worked out well. By then, I had a job as a chemist, and she had time to do all the planning. Since she picked the month, I picked the day. I didn't want to wait, so I picked April 1, a Saturday. If it didn't work out, we could just say, "April fools'!" (Joking, of course.)

It was during that period of planning and preparation that I realized just how well we balanced each other out. I've always been great at organizing, but hated detail work. Thankfully, Crystal excelled at details. She would get nervous and upset when things didn't work out, but I could calm her down and refocus her.

One evening, she called me crying, frustrated because she couldn't find a place for our reception. She was working within a budget, but had saved enough to afford more than a gymnasium. I told her not to worry about the reception hall, and that I would take care of it.

My parents and I dined out frequently, and I knew many restaurants which offered banquet rooms. So, I found a couple of options at my favorite restaurants. After a few visits and some negotiation, the choice became obvious.

The Rosewood Inn in Blue Island, Illinois had the perfect classy room, and could provide a nice family-style meal within Crystal's budget. There was room for a quartet, an adequate dance floor, and our hundred and twenty guests. When I told Crystal, I could feel her love and appreciation over the phone. When I showed her the room, it earned me a big wet one, with the promise of many more to come.

Crystal had tried to talk me into a later date in April, because the weather in Chicago could go either way April 1st. I, however, promised it would be 60 degrees and sunny. Well, God must have agreed with me. The day before our wedding, the forecast called for party cloudy skies with a high between 58 and 62 degrees. To prove it was a miracle, the weatherman actually wound up being correct.

One more hurdle complicated the matter, though. On Easter Sunday a week before our wedding, Crystal was admitted to the hospital after suffering abdominal problems. It turned out to be a gynecological issue. This was the first time I realized that women are the unlucky gender when it comes to health problems. She had one of those common but treatable conditions. Of course, she was afraid we would have to postpone the wedding.

I told Crystal we would still get married, even in the hospital if necessary. I think my resolve surprised everyone, including Crystal. Her father didn't care much for my attitude, but he knew how much I cared for Crystal.

To everyone's amazement, the focus shifted. They stopped questioning what to do. The question became not if, but how. How can we get Crystal to the wedding? Thankfully, the medicine started working, and Crystal started feeling better. Even the nurses were dedicated to helping her get out of bed. She was released two days before the wedding. She could walk, but lacked energy.

April 1st arrived bright and sunny—a beautiful day to get married. I had been calm until the big day. I felt nervous during the ride to Faith United Methodist Church in Dolton, Illinois, but I knew that everything would be fine once I saw my best man, Dominic, and groomsmen, Larry, Perry, Corky, and Wayne. They were encouraging, and told me Crystal had arrived on time in her dress, and most importantly, wasn't in pain.

My parents arrived and were positive, although I think my mother would have been just as happy if I had moved back home. After all, I was her baby. Crystal's father had a similar reaction. In fact, right before he walked Crystal down the aisle, he mentioned it wasn't too late for her to change her mind. Crystal calmly brushed it off.

I would have resented the implication; except I knew where our parents were coming from. Now as a father, who has given away a couple of daughters, I understand the feeling of loss. When you raise a child, you invest part of yourself in the process. It takes time to adapt to the idea, that someone has taken your place in your child's heart, but you eventually realize your child's love for you never fades.

Once Crystal entered the sanctuary with her dad, I felt a little queasy. My mind raced with thoughts about the permanency of the commitment, and even disbelief that, the moment was finally at hand. Crystal did look beautiful in her in her bright white floor length A-line dress, with a long train edged in lace and beads. She wore a Juliet style veil that she had made. Crystal and her mother had designed the dress. It was made with love, lace, and more than a thousand beads, each sewn on by hand. Indeed, it was a work of art. Crystal's mom had made a lot of her wardrobe throughout most of her life, and taught Crystal to sew as well.

Crystal was smiling, and would have scampered down the aisle if her father hadn't slightly restrained her. I was sure that everyone was watching her, but Jeannette was watching me. She later yelled at me for looking anxious, and not smiling. By the time Crystal made it to the altar, my nervousness dissipated. As I took her hand, everything felt right again. This was the person I loved, and would be with forever. A few steps down the aisle had changed that thought, from a threat to a promise.

The ceremony was fairly short, about 20 minutes, but tasteful. I still remember the reading about trees growing close, but not in each other's shadows. To this day, we've never had that problem. Our mutual support and encouragement have helped keep us together.

Our Wedding Party, Left to right, Corky Kahn, Debbie Maat, Larry Rose, Dorothy Toren, Dominic Francone, Crystal, Ron, Jeannette Carlson, Larry Carlson, Kathy Beech, Wayne Anderson, and Perry Miyashita on April 1, 1978, at Faith United Methodist Church in Dolton, Il.

I've never had more fun at a reception than my own. The food was great. There was roast beef, manicotti, and sausage with sauerkraut, accompanied by salad and bread. Everyone danced. We hired a band that played waltzes, polkas, rock and roll and more. I think at one time or another everyone ventured onto the dance floor. The band even played some of our fraternity favorites like Rock Around the Clock. Our college friends and fraternity brothers and sisters partied especially hard. By the time we said goodbye, the plastic Champagne glasses had piled up on a table about four or five rows high.

While everything went perfectly on April first, April 2nd didn't start out as well. I literally slid out to my car the next day. I had to chip about a quarter-inch coat of ice off my windshield. What a miserable day in Chicago. I would have preferred six inches of snow than the wet, frigid, windy day. Thank goodness we were leaving on our honeymoon.

It was slow going to O'Hare airport. I had flown plenty, but this was Crystal's first flight. To say she was nervous would have been an understatement. She turned pale in the airport, darting her eyes back and forth. I tried to reassure her, but had to resort to plan B. I ordered her a frozen, but potent drink in the lounge. Before she knew, we were on the plane. Mimosas appeared after I mentioned our honeymoon to the stewardess.

When we arrived at the Tucson airport in Arizona, Crystal's nervousness returned. A lot of people are afraid to fly. However, Crystal is the only one I know who likes flying, but is frightened of airports. She later shared that, not only was she afraid of the airport, but also realized she was going a long way from home.

Thankfully, in Tucson, we saw no trace of the ice storm we had left. It was 80 degrees and sunny with palm trees and blooming cactuses. Finally, Crystal relaxed. She knew she had made the right decision to marry me.

We bonded as we toured Tucson, Phoenix, and the Grand Canyon. I introduced Crystal to Mexican food, and we played tennis, hiked, swam, and rode horses. I still think of those eight days as some of our best times together. Those memories have helped us both through many challenging times.

Crystal and Ron during their honeymoon at the Grand Canyon in Arizona in April 1978.

It takes a lot of compromise and survival skills to make a marriage work. We realize we didn't get here on our own. That's why we dedicated the rest of this book to our parents.

II

Maria and Siegfried

Ron

Like a lot of kids, I grew up knowing little about my parents' histories prior to God's greatest gift—me—entering their lives. Sometimes they tried to share stories, but I wasn't interested. All that mattered was they were loving parents. However, as an adult and a father myself, I felt somehow compelled to learn about my roots.

My parents had a connection that couldn't be broken. Their relationship seemed always in flux, between their obvious love and stress. Today, after studying them though time, I think I have at least some insight. We are all reflections of what we experience in life, good or bad. We cope with challenges in the least painful way. When coping is no longer possible in the conventional or accepted ways, we form defense mechanisms, or escape reality in other ways. I see now what I couldn't as a child.

My parents were traumatized as children and young adults. My father only recently disclosed his psychotic breakdown a few years after the war ended. He was still recovering in 1954. In March of that year his father died. A few weeks later I was born. Three days after that his mother committed suicide. He still regrets not being able to offer her support due to his condition. Around the same time, he was recalled to active duty for the Korean War; although he never went due to his personal, and medical issues. Today a lot is known about PTSD in its many forms. In the 1940s and 1950s, the many thousands of returning veterans with those types of problems weren't properly diagnosed or treated.

While I never noticed any abnormalities with dad as I grew, mom's struggles were ongoing. I couldn't have imagined what my mother endured. As I grew up, she suffered emotional difficulties, with paranoia and delusions. Much of the time she was functional and symptom free. At times, however, she couldn't help but retreat from reality. This could occur randomly, or be brought on by stress or a comment. From an early age, I had to explain her oddities, such as peering through the window at school, or accusing a neighbor of sticking me with pins to control me. Thankfully, most people were very understanding. I took on my dad's pragmatic tone when explaining her eccentricities to neighbors or teachers. I would say things like, mom has some problems, but she is harmless. That was usually all they wanted to know.

In one of her delusions, she claimed she was born a princess, but was abducted at a railway station at the age of three, by the people who ended up raising her. I have tried to research this story with no success. If anyone lost a princess in 1927, please let me know.

While I considered both of my parents intelligent, my mother never thought of herself that way. Despite her challenges, she did well at school. I fear that part of her abuse was being repeatedly called stupid by her father. Eventually, a child believes what they're told, and may be irreparably damaged by it.

While she was emotional and people oriented, my father was an intellectual and frequently avoided unnecessary interactions. My mother took her role as wife and mother to extremes, and tended to our every need. In contrast, my father relaxed by reading technical articles and work papers between dinner and the late news. He could be particularly obtuse to my mother's emotional arguments. While their conflicts rarely became physical, I remember one dream where my mom stabbed dad with a kitchen knife. It was one of the only dreams I ever had in color. I became a good mediator, but it took a toll on me, especially as an only child, having no-one with whom to share this role. My sense of humor also usually helped diffuse their tension.

I've always felt blessed for my parents and my upbringing, but I worried they might not stay together when I left for college. However, the depth of their bond was far deeper than I had perceived. They shared a culture, and the struggles of growing up in a depressed, post-World War One Germany. They had to deal with vast changes as the new regime slowly and methodically rose to power. They weathered the stress of adapting to a new society in America, and never stopped evolving their ways of thinking and acting.

This is the story, as they recounted, of those life-shaping times and experiences.

HITLER ON PARADE

My parents grew up in some of the most tumultuous times in German history. After World War I, the world punished Germany. President Woodrow Wilson had enough forethought to provide a plan, with his Fourteen Points, which might have assisted Germany, and the other devastated countries in their recovery. The goal: a closer, better structured world community.

However, the rest of the free world did not view post WW1 Germany in a similar light. Wilson was voted down. It was decided that Germany hadn't suffered enough for its role as instigator. Severe financial, social, and military restrictions sought to control the German population and prevent a similar aggression from ever occurring again.

Just as excessive use of negative discipline is counterproductive in raising well-adjusted children, the same can be said of countries and cultures. As with children, this type of severe punishment is only effective short term. Unlike children, who can be scarred by abuse, a country, with a long-standing heritage of pride and accomplishment will do anything to reestablish its legacy.

My father, Siegfried Meinstein, was born November 15, 1920, in Zirndorf, Germany. I will never forget my visit to the small northern Bavarian town around 1965 at age eleven. His old red two-story brick house on a cobblestone street still appeared well kept. I imagine it looked much the same as in the twenties when my dad was a boy. It was a typical European street scene, with houses at least a century old, slate shingled roofs, lined rather close together. The city was mainly flat, surrounded by rolling hills, farmland, and forested areas.

A stroll through the town's graveyard gave me a real sense of heritage. At least eighty Meinsteins and relatives were buried there, marked by simple stones. Farther back, the dates became earlier and earlier, and the names harder and harder to read; erosion had erased them beyond legibility prior to the eighteenth century. Having met few Meinsteins, I finally knew that, my roots were deeply German, at least through my father.

Growing up, Siegfried was keen to his heritage. He and his younger brother, Max, lived with their parents Louis and Rosa Meinstein (Formerly Rosa Kimmelstiel), maternal grandmother, Jeanette Rosenbaum, paternal grandfather, Hermann Meinstein, and a maid. Life was much like it was in the mid eighteen-hundreds in the United States. The pace of life was slow, with few modern conveniences, such as central heating or electrical appliances. The lack of what we consider necessities today created an almost endless list of chores. However, dad felt that relationships were stronger, and life seemed less stressful and often more satisfying and rewarding.

There was no sexual revolution; roles were gender specific and well understood. Women cleaned, cooked, knitted, mended, and shined shoes (To date, I've never been able to talk Crystal into darning one sock. Once, she said, "Darn sock," and handed it back to me). Life back then was fraught with hard work. Breaks had to be planned. Siegfried's mother caught up on the town gossip weekly at a café.

His father found his cattle brokerage business socially fulfilling. He purchased animals from local farmers, and negotiated the best prices at city markets. He rode a bicycle or drove a rented car to the farms in neighboring villages, and enjoyed leisurely conversations while buying their cattle. He transported the livestock by train, and employed a cowhand to move the cattle to his holding stables in Zirndorf. Cattle were sold weekly in Nuremberg and other larger neighboring livestock markets.

The weekends afforded days of devotion and relaxation. The Meinsteins hardly ever missed synagogue services Friday evenings and Saturday mornings. They walked in the woods, stopped at favorite cafes, visited with friends, played card games, and watched local soccer games. They also enjoyed seasonal, traditional entertainment, such as village fairs, carnivals, and Fasching, also known as *Karneval.*

I can certainly attest to the Germans' love of parties. Each time I visited in the 1960s and 1970s, fairs or events with music, dancing, games, food, and of course, beer were everywhere. When I was fifteen, my conservative parents had no problem with me indulging in a beer or two at one such event. After all, we were in Germany! At home, they debated whether I should have one sip of New Year's Eve Champagne.

Although Zirndorf had less than ten thousand people, community events and family activities were abundant. My father believed his parents knew most of the established families in the community.

The Meinsteins, along with twenty-five to thirty other families, were members of the Jewish community in semirural Zirndorf. Until 1933, religion and nationality never conflicted, nor were they in the least incompatible. My father, as he put it, was raised as a German by conviction, and just happened to be of the Jewish faith. They were Germans, pure and simple. His ancestors had lived within one hundred miles of picturesque, sleepy little Zirndorf, as far back as medieval times according to memory.

His grandfather Hermann talked with enormous pride of his service in the Bavarian Cavalry Division of the Royal Bavarian Army, under the first German Kaiser. His eyes lit up as he described his army exploits after the Franco-Prussian War. Despite his chronic lung disease, that had emaciated him at seventy-five years old, he straightened up in his chair to sing an old soldier's war ditty or two at his grandsons' urging.

A life-sized painting of him on horseback in his colorful cavalry uniform, complete with plumed helmet and saber, hung in the corner of the sitting room. It was a daily reminder of his esteemed service. Similarly, my father's maternal grandmother, Jeanette, made history come to life with her stories of harboring Bavarian soldiers during the Austro-Prussian War of 1866.

Siegfried's dad was not left out when it came to serving his country. He would proudly reconstruct his WWI experiences as a German soldier on the Russian front. In glowing terms, he would describe Field Marshal Paul von Hindenburg's master stroke during the Battle of Tannenberg in 1914, which among other things, saved his unit of army engineers.

The Meinsteins did not escape their roles in the German armies unscathed. Siegfried's father busted an eardrum from artillery fire, and his grandfather lost two sons on the stalemated western front. Both refused compensation from the German government.

I find it ironic that our family, and others like it, were singled out in the late 1930s as the cause of Germany's faded glory, and diminished world prominence.

While religion and heritage may have been prominent in Adolf Hitler's mind, my father and his younger brother weren't conscious of religious barriers in their early lives. They attended a local Catholic kindergarten and participated in Christmas plays. I remember being mildly surprised as a child. Dad knew all of the words to "Silent Night" in German.

The strictness and discipline of German life started early. In elementary school, the training for proper politeness and respect for others accompanied the three Rs of reading, writing, and arithmetic. The teacher's dreaded hickory stick reinforced these important life lessons. Perhaps because of, perhaps in spite of such strict discipline, Siegfried learned his lessons well.

Siegfried's soccer team dressed in lederhosen in Fürth, Germany, circa 1930. He was the favorite of the coach whose left hand is on his shoulder.

After school and on weekends, he roamed the woods with friends and played cops and robbers (or soldiers) around the fortification remnants of the Thirty Years' War. Siegfried also excelled on the junior soccer team.

He grew up rather pleasantly, with no worries and few cares. In the backdrop, however, political discussions were heating up. A beer hall across the yard from the family's living room hosted local meetings. Julius Streicher, a high-profile Nazi, and other anti-Semitic speakers periodically appeared in town. Their message and its destructive potential escaped Siegfried's and many others' understanding. However, the colorful parades of all description thrilled them.

Occasionally, Siegfried's mother would take her sons to the charming trading center of Nuremberg. A mere six-mile trip led to opportunities to explore the town with a castle and moat, Gothic architecture, prominent churches, and historical fountains and public buildings. Supposedly, the Brothers Grimm published much of the folktales about the tiny dwellings in this medieval setting. On the outskirts of town, a lake served as a perfect backdrop for the zoo and African tribesmen performing their traditional dances.

Once his mom finished her shopping, they enjoyed pastries, and an afternoon variety show at a café, or freshwater fish at one of the wood-paneled old kitchens along the Pegnitz River.

Even as life seemed so good and the future so promising, changes were stirring. In Nuremberg when he was six, Siegfried begged his mother to watch the marching columns of a summer parade in 1927. They mingled with the crowd that lined the narrow, winding streets. A spectator explained, it was a relatively new fanatical extremist group that was in town for a political party gathering.

Siegfried's mom was blond, which was unusual for Jewish people. And when she asked one of the uniformed Nazi crowd-control soldiers to give Siegfried a better vantage point for the parade, he hoisted her son onto his shoulders. Generally, spectators of these parades appeared merely curious instead of enthused. Yet, to Siegfried, it felt momentous with the brass bands, fife and drum corps, brown uniforms, mysterious flags, hobnailed boots striking the cobblestones in unison, chants, and upraised arms.

The only man, not wearing a cap, stood stiffly in an open car. He appeared solemn as he slowly raised his right arm, bent at the elbow, with his open hand facing forward. In contrast, members of the marching columns raised their right arms briskly and stiffly at an angle in front of them in unison. Though it was rumored the man in the car with a slight mustache was the leader (fuhrer), Siegfried thought he was the least impressive aspect of the colorful parade.

Siegfried saw other parades in Nuremburg, including two in 1930 for Fasching and President Hindenburg's birthday. The common themes were extensive military processions, multicolored floats, bands, and extensive length.

While not as long, parades in Zirndorf were more plentiful. At the sound of a trumpet or drums, Siegfried and his friends dashed off to find them. They didn't care about their political or national agenda. It didn't matter if they were the Social Democratic Party, Nazis, firefighters, first-aid men, foresters, or hunters. Siegfried's uncle, a bald man of rather large stature, participated as a bass drummer in a WWI veteran's parade. He later died in a concentration camp.

In late 1932, political rallies and parades turned more serious. The aged and failing conservative German government opened the door to more extreme points of view. Occasionally in parades, fisticuffs ensued between right- and left-wing extremists. To his parents' dismay, Siegfried and his friends considered it added entertainment value. In retrospect, he feels lucky he was never struck by a stray blow or projectile.

Despite the far-reaching political upheaval, the everyday quiet, slow pace of life seemed to continue. From Siegfried's point of view, much local sentiment was against the Nazis gaining an election victory at any cost. However, probably a majority, including his parents, were politically apathetic. A variety of political parties in power had faltered in the recent past. Why not let the Nazis try when they too probably would falter? The Germans were tired of groups' empty promises after rising to power. They wanted somebody, anybody, who could extract Germany from its deep-rooted depression. However, the apathy led to low voter turnouts, and political discussion was scarce in little Zirndorf. Children found rivalries of neighboring soccer teams far more interesting to follow.

Everything changed, though, on that fateful day of January 30, 1933. That was when President Hindenburg appointed Hitler as chancellor of Germany. Siegfried and most Zirndorfers considered this just an excuse for a more elaborate parade. As most of the townspeople enjoyed the torch lighting and victory celebration, no one could predict this seemingly innocuous election would soon change the course of life in Germany, and most of the civilized world, forever.

Childhood in Germany

It's human nature to want your parents to come from a happy childhood. Unfortunately, my mother had a lot to overcome; some of which, she never could.

Maria Liegl was born September 12, 1924, to a poor family in a suburb of Munich. She lived with her mother Maria, father Michael, and younger brother Josef in a dank, smelly one-bedroom house with a low ceiling and no running water or electricity.

The main room measured about sixteen by sixteen feet with a couch, table, and small kitchen. There were two small bed areas and a narrow hallway. Maria and her brother shared a bed. They used an outhouse and a toilet in the hall, which they flushed by pouring pumped water down it.

When Maria was around five years old, the family moved to Feldmoching district in the northern part of Munich. She carried a kerosene lantern to school during her first couple of years.

Children had to quickly learn their place in Germany's strict culture of discipline, and do what was expected of them—without questions. The lines between discipline and abuse were obscured. No one was allowed to complain or seek help.

A lot of Germans were poor, but her crude, ill-tempered father exacerbated their situation. He always seemed to be in a dark mood when he wasn't lifting loads, and assisting bakers at a flour mill. The family suffered for it. He beat Maria multiple times each week, and she frequently trudged to school with bruises, black eyes, and sore ribs. Her mother tried to protect her children, but was beaten too. He began touching Maria inappropriately as early as first grade, and his abuse persisted throughout her youth.

Maria Liegl around five years old 1929 or 30.

Their new home was in a semi-rural suburban setting. Maria liked the country, though she had to walk almost an hour each way for school. The three-bedroom house was nothing extravagant, but it was relatively new. Maria had her own room. It was barely large enough for her bed and a small cabinet, but at least she had some privacy.

When she was nine, her family could afford to begin building a home close to their rental, thanks to a government initiative. Maria worked as hard as the men as she moved stones, fetched water, and stirred the concrete. The first year, they lived in the four-room basement. When it rained, water ran down the interior walls. Still, it felt like a home. When complete the house was still quite small although Mom never gave me any real details.

While no one tried to rescue Maria's family from her father's abuse, many helped as much as they could. Maria was well liked. In fact, a teacher even visited her at home when she was sick—quite an honor.

Whenever they could, townspeople gave her hand-me-downs. However, she still had to wear shoes with holes or go barefoot. One winter, her feet were so frostbitten that her father rubbed them with snow—the treatment back then. Maria believed it saved her feet, but the circulation in her hands and feet was poor the rest of her life. Her hands almost always had a white-blue cast.

Maria recalled that as she grew, one of the greatest challenges was finding enough food. She insisted that she seldom went hungry. Maria gorged on raspberries on their property when they were in season. The socialist government made some food available, such as milk at the consumer's union. Occasionally, the whole town smelled like fish when it was brought in… or a rather strong cheese when it was distributed.

The town baker offered broken cookies and bread to children—his donation in those tough times. Maria's mother would get a bargain price for his slightly outdated or imperfect goods. In fact, Maria suspected that he ruined some of it on purpose to help out. Her mom would spread them on the table, so Maria and her brother could eat all they wanted. For them, it was like Christmas.

On the outskirts of town, they rented a small garden and part of a barn. This allowed them to grow vegetables such as turnips, potatoes and radishes, which lasted most of the year. Home canning was a fall family activity. Maria's brother raised rabbits in the barn. Maria looked forward to a rabbit dinner almost every Sunday. When I was young, she cooked rabbit for me. Unfortunately, all I could think about was Bugs Bunny. I ate a couple of bites, which I found disgusting. Maria also got a job helping raise and tending for some goats, in the same barn and nearby pastures. For her efforts, she was paid mainly in milk, and occasionally goat meat.

Around 1934, when Maria was ten, teachers at her Catholic-based school started to talk about Hitler, and the new Germany, during the hour usually dedicated to religious studies.

Every young person was required to join the Hitler Youth, and a youth leader came to the house when Maria missed some meetings because she was sick. He yelled at her parents about her duty to the fatherland. After that, her father, who belonged to the Communist Party, forbid her from attending again. As a result, her friends ostracized her at school, until their teacher lectured them on how everyone is valuable in society.

Although she was never again forced to join the Hitler Youth or Nazi Party, she did her part in building the

German army. Between the ages of fourteen and sixteen, she made horse cakes. You don't see much of it in the old war movies, but the German army relied on horses to move men and supplies. So, three nights a week, Maria helped form and wrap masses of compressed hay and grains, designed for easy transport, to sustain those horses.

Maria's other job was taking the goats out to the fields every day to graze. When she was fourteen, she climbed into a hunting blind while the goats ate. Absorbed in peace, she didn't notice the SS troops maneuvering around the field.

When the war games erupted with shooting, the goats scattered and Maria jumped down without a thought to run after them. The soldiers stopped shooting, and one stern-looking officer walked up to Maria, who was terrified. He stared at her while trying not to grin and said, "Thanks to you and your goats, the German army has lost the war."

Any activities not related to the Nazi regime became less and less tolerated. No place was immune, including school and church. In 1938, Nazis with sticks invaded her father's Communist Party meeting. He was detained in an internment camp for six weeks. After that, there was no more talk about communism.

Maria graduated high school at seventeen, and got a job at the air force technical school. It was a rather high-security facility, where airplane design work and records were prepared and stored. Certain rooms were off limits, and plans were covered up. She typed technical reports, though she seldom understood all the engineering jargon. She had to be accurate, because there was no quick way to correct mistakes.

In 1942 when she was eighteen, the war was in full swing, but Germany was not yet under attack. Her parents finally divorced. A month later her father was remarried. Soon after, both he and Maria's brother were drafted. It was only about six months later; they were informed that both had been killed on the Eastern front. Maria was devastated about her brother, but as much as she tried, she never really grieved for her father.

She and her mother moved to a country town of around 500 known as Reichenberg, about sixty miles from Munich. This was to be her last home in Germany. Maria quickly got a job at the Airforce Training school, a short train or bike ride away. She worked there until near the end of the war.

The six-year war ended when she was twenty-one years old—a double milestone. Finally, she embarked on a better chapter of her life.

Despite her difficult childhood, Maria grew into a lovely young lady. Her pictures look like she could have modeled for magazines. In her early twenties, soon after the war (1947), a friend introduced her to an Austrian artist named R. Strudel. He felt compelled to paint her portrait. Mom told me he had, in his youth, been a primary painter for Bavarian royalty and aristocracy. The painting followed dad when we moved him to Ohio, and was proudly displayed in each of his residences. After his death I had it reframed for our home.

When I was about six or seven, my parents and I met two sets of Mom's aunts and uncles in Germany—one in Munich, the other in Straubing. I will never forget their greetings, and the emotions of these people who had last seen me as a baby. There were hugs, tears, and kisses like we had just escaped death.

Strudel's portrait of Maria.

They treated me like a prince; nothing was to be denied to me. While I tried to remain humble, I was fascinated by a valuable coin collection owned by Mom's uncle in Straubing. He insisted I take it. I believe he might have cried if I had refused. I still have it, along with the memories.

Only recently did I realize their emotional outpouring was not for me, but for my mom. When she was young, she visited her relatives regularly. I'm sure they had some insight into her hardships, and were thankful to see she had blossomed into a healthy wife and mother.

Coming to America

Under significant intimidation and coercion, elections were held in March 1933, at the insistence of Chancellor Hitler, to assure the Nazi stronghold. More than 40 percent of voters refused to be swayed by strong-arm polling tactics, and voted against the new regime.

For the remainder of his life, Siegfried blamed the ignorance of the men at World War I's Treaty of Versailles for opening the door to Hitler.

Changes at local levels gradually became obvious after the election—or staged performance, as Siegfried called it. Placard-carrying SA men enforced boycotts of non-Aryan establishments. Some people, including Siegfried's uncle, were sent to the new concentration camps for short (between a couple of weeks to several months) periods of "protective custody." Some villages posted signs stating 'Jews Not Wanted Here.'

Yet to Siegfried, those signs seemed little more personal than the typical slurs amongst children. When some of his friends joined the Nazi junior youth group, his biggest regret was that he couldn't join, wear a uniform, and go on hikes.

Siegfried was an enthusiastic spectator later that year, when uniformed Nazi troops arrived in Nuremberg, to participate in the annual rally, called Reichsparteitag. At such events, he remembers singing patriotic German songs, and even raising his right hand along with the crowd. He was particularly impressed with the National Socialist Flying Corps, precursor to the Luftwaffe. An overflow of Nazi Party enthusiasts cheered on the demonstration, which included a fleet of mainly light civilian planes bombing a community of cardboard buildings at a neighboring airport

Thus, to the children, the first year of the new Third Reich was little more than an excuse to attend a series of patriotic, colorful events. Siegfried's folks, however, began to feel the effects of strangling, hateful economic and social restrictions. With a sense of what was to come, they began to formulate a plan to send Siegfried to his Uncle Max and Aunt Audrey Meinstein in America.

Siegfried thought the trip to a new life in America sounded like a rare adventure. After all, in his thirteen years of life, he had never traveled more that seventy-five miles from his birthplace. Any journey more than fifteen miles had been a memorable event. This, however, would be a voyage to the other side of the Earth, and to—of all places—America! Adding to the excitement, his uncle and aunt lived in Chicago!

He had formed many impressions of America from books, movies, and hearsay from his elders. It was the land of skyscrapers, actors Tom Mix and Hoot Gibson, cowboys and Indians, and limitless possibilities. It was a wealthy land, with richly upholstered automobiles, and new foods and candies, some of which visiting relatives had brought him to taste.

Yes, he was destined for intense, awe-inspiring Chicago, known for bad boys Al Capone and John Dillinger, and daily gunfire between gangs and police. It was a city where no unarmed residents could go about their daily business without endangering their lives. I personally witnessed this perception, long after its reality faded. For example, when we visited Germany in the 1960s, kids imitated machine-gun noise when we mentioned our hometown. I had to ask my mom to explain it to me.

The eight-day ship journey to America alone was an adventure in Itself. Siegfried had heard numerous stories about the dangers of traveling over the bottomless ocean. Back in the 1850s, his grandfather was marooned near an iceberg for three weeks, while crossing the Atlantic in a sailing vessel. They had all but run out of supplies before a shift in the wind saved them.

An emigrating acquaintance of his parents accompanied Siegfried to his new homeland. His parents stayed behind to care for his grandparents in their old age. When Siegfried arrived, the skyscrapers and bustling city were just as he had imagined.

While his aunt and uncle were loving and well-adjusted to life in America, they could only do so much to help him adapt. A growing prejudice against Germany and almost anything German in the U.S. didn't help. However, Siegfried eventually learned to fit in. Usually, sports can serve as a social opportunity, but his athleticism on the soccer field took a while to translate to baseball and American football.

School in America was a culture shock. He couldn't believe the lack of discipline and disrespect! His aptitude and love of learning impressed his teachers. Even as he was learning the language, he found himself way ahead for his level. He easily completed his assignments, and had time to help his uncle at work. Uncle Max had a thriving live poultry business on Chicago's South Water Street. They supplied fresh poultry to many restaurants in Chicago. Uncle Max once confided in me he was proud of the fact that, Chicago's China Town almost exclusively trusted only his business for their live poultry.

In his relatively small amount of leisure time, Siegfried enjoyed going to the movies, which featured the newsreels. The brief summaries of local and world events were dominated by the "war in Europe." Siegfried watched with great interest, disappointment, and anger. The laissez-faire attitude of post WWI America was frustrating. He knew, well before most, that only decisive, united action could stem the tide of the tyranny, which was soon to engulf all of Europe and beyond. He had grown up hearing the tales of his family's glorious contributions to German military history. Would his turn ever come? His answer was not far off.

But life in Chicago was not without its own adventures. On July 22, 1934, he went with a couple of friends to the Biograph Theater, near Lincoln Park for a double feature. One of the movies was about Chicago gangsters. Later that evening, and for days after, they ended up returning to the Biograph to look over a crime scene, and search for any embedded bullets. Unlike today, where police tape would impede the youths, only blood stains marked the event. A couple of hours after their double feature, J. Edgar Hoover's newly established Federal Bureau of Investigation had shot and killed gangster John Dillinger, during a firefight in the theater's alley. Siegfried claims they did indeed dig out some stray bullets.

In 1936, his parents in Germany arranged for his younger brother's emigration before they finally arrived in the autumn of 1938. Relieved as they were to escape the escalating persecution, they were overwhelmed by culture shock. While they never forgot their values or their friends, the Old-World pace, and leisure time spent shopping or relaxing at cafes became only memories.

This longing was compounded by the loss of most of their furniture and worldly possessions. Although some friends had promised to ship their belongings after their departure, the goods fell prey to the torch of a radical group of fanatical, brown-shirted youths. This happened on an infamous night, called Kristallnacht, or Night of Broken Glass, in November 1938, when violence against Jews was stoked to retaliate for a Polish Jew assassinating a German diplomat in Paris. It marked the beginning of organized, mass acts of brutality against Jews, and any remaining opponents of the so-called New Germany.

If Siegfried's parents had waited any longer to flee, their loss might have been more than just furniture. Siegfried's father had fought and lost two brothers in the last world war. With the shaking of a madman's hand, all of that meant nothing now. It was time to leave. Still, when all seemed lost, there was still hope.

Compared to life in Germany, the daily pace in Chicago seemed to zoom at supersonic speed. There were unaccustomed luxuries, such as hot and cold running water, steam heat, gas ovens, built-in closets, and wall-to-wall carpeting. On the other hand, they missed the spaciousness and high ceilings of their Old-World home, which afforded bedrooms for the boys rather than a sofa bed in the living room, a yard, and privacy. It had been a two-family house, as opposed to the thirty-family apartment complex.

Siegfried's parents found jobs rather quickly—his father as a restaurant dishwasher, and his mother a seamstress. While his mom had excellent sewing skills, she was unaccustomed to the rigors of working at it full time. Wife and mother was always a respected calling in Germany. They had to adjust to the hustling, bustling crowds, and traffic-laden streets, with fast-stopping streetcars and elevated trains. They had only a short lunch break and then back to work! This was a stark contrast to the one- to two-hour leisurely meals back in Europe.

After work, they rushed home for a quickly prepared, but substantial meal. Household chores loomed before an early bedtime. Housekeeping, laundry, and ironing consumed the weekends. The lack of fresh air and never-ending city noises exacerbated an ongoing sense of fatigue.

Indeed, the old ways were gone, but Siegfried and his family were grateful for their safety and new start. Through hard work, they became self-sufficient, and Siegfried took advantage of the opportunities. His discipline and intellect helped him shine among his fellow students.

In 1938, he became one of the very few students in the country to receive a full academic scholarship to the prestigious University of Chicago. With little spare time, he continued to work part time during the school year, and full-time during breaks.

Somehow, though, he found time to once again play his favorite sport. Soccer came back to him as if he had never stopped playing. It served as a release from the pressure of his studies and hard work at his uncle's business.

He graduated with a bachelor's degree in chemistry, and a varsity letter from the soccer team.

Counter Intelligence

Siegfried's busy schedule didn't isolate him from world events. While still in college, Siegfried was enmeshed in the growing conflict overseas. He, better than most Americans, understood the immense threat of a world war. He was determined to help. Inspired by movie newsreels, during his break between his sophomore and junior year, he wrote a letter to the British High Command. The letter detailed a strategy to reduce the effectiveness of the German dive bombers, used in the early blitzkrieg of London, and other British targets. Based on newsreel pictures detailing attacks, he proposed that British planes could drag netting to snare the bombers during the raids.

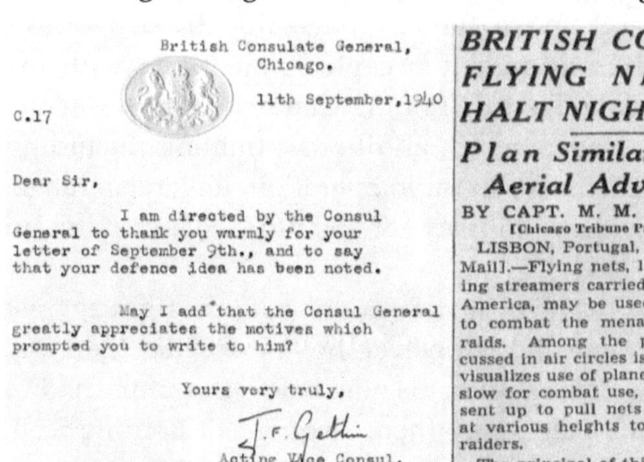

British Consulate General,
Chicago.

11th September, 1940

C.17

Dear Sir,

I am directed by the Consul General to thank you warmly for your letter of September 9th., and to say that your defence idea has been noted.

May I add that the Consul General greatly appreciates the motives which prompted you to write to him?

Yours very truly,

J. F. Gethin

Acting Vice Consul.

Mr. S. Meinstein,
541 Wellington Avenue,
Chicago.

JFG:rl

BRITISH CONSIDER FLYING NETS TO HALT NIGHT RAIDS

Plan Similar to U. S. Aerial Advertising.

BY CAPT. M. M. CORPENING.
[Chicago Tribune Press Service.]

LISBON, Portugal, Dec. 18 [By Air Mail].—Flying nets, like the advertising streamers carried by airplanes in America, may be used by the British to combat the menace of night air raids. Among the plans being discussed in air circles is a system which visualizes use of planes considered too slow for combat use, which would be sent up to pull nets back and forth at various heights to enmesh enemy raiders.

The principal of this plan is similar to the advertising streamers seen by Americans at public gatherings, except on a vastly larger scale.

Siegfried Meinstein's keepsakes from his scrapbooks.

The British Consulate General responded with a letter of appreciation for his idea, which may have led to a similar strategy with balloons. While this proved only marginally effective, it was part of the multifaceted defense strategy, that eventually led to the victory in Great Britain.

The attack on Pearl Harbor occurred in the middle of his junior year, inciting the U.S. military to act. Overnight, the U.S. apathy and isolationist attitude were replaced by anger, determination, and resolve.

Only a few days after his college graduation, Siegfried volunteered to take part in the greatest adventure of his life. Indeed, he had been destined to continue his family's fine military tradition—but with an ironic twist. He would fight on the other side, against Germany and the Axis powers.

It felt like the U.S. army had been waiting for him. Not only was Siegfried college educated, but he also was thoroughly versed in the geography and culture of Germany, and spoke the language fluently. An officer training program quickly accepted him, along with the U.S. Army Intelligence Training Center at Camp Ritchie, Maryland. He received additional training including consolidated courses in radio operation, Italian language, and intelligence courses at Stanford University in California.

On some level, it was tough to aid the fight against his native homeland. However, he knew better than any of his fellow officers that, his new beloved country had to stop the Nazi plague. By then, Siegfried fit in quite well. He spoke fluent English with only a trace of an accent, and had absorbed American culture. He even chimed in when someone insulted the dirty krauts.

After his training in February 1944, he was sent to the United Kingdom, where he taught German army organization, including weapons, to company grade officers in Northern Ireland and England's Midlands. In June, he reveled in the success of the D-Day invasion in Normandy, France, realizing the significant strategic advantage gained.

In September 1944, he was assigned to the Counter Intelligence Corps (CIC) in France, and attached to the 83rd Infantry Division's 331st Regiment. He remained with the 83rd until the end of the war, and participated in three major campaigns: Central Europe, Battle of the Bulge, and Rhineland.

To accomplish his main objective of gathering intelligence about German operations, his group needed to identify, seek, and capture enemy agents left behind by retreating German army units. They worked with local collaborators, and interrogated German prisoners to glean information about the German forces and strategies. Although under orders, his unit had a little more freedom than most. From their division's base, they moved on their own, from the frontlines to behind the lines, to best fulfill their main objective.

While every person in a uniform had some effect and honorable role in the war, few individuals were in a position to significantly change history. Siegfried had one such opportunity. While his efforts fell short, the story is a good one just the same.

For Americans, the Battle of the Bulge was the largest and bloodiest battle of World War II. The initial assault took American and British forces by surprise. In this case, though, surprise is somewhat of a nebulous word, and a question of perspective. My dad tells the story the best:

> Around Thanksgiving of 1944, my CIC unit and I performed our mission in Luxembourg City for about one week. For several days, two agents and I lived in a requisitioned house close to the Moselle River, which was the frontline. As we roamed the area, a couple of infantry GIs brought us three captured German soldiers wearing wet uniforms. They apparently had swum across the Moselle and surrendered to us.
>
> In my interrogation of these three guys around twenty years old, they alleged to be Luxembourgers who were drafted into the German army after Hitler's troops overran Luxembourg in 1940. The small country was annexed into the German Reich. It was obvious these young men were just happy to get home. They told me about a large buildup of armor and artillery in the last couple days.
>
> In my report, which ultimately reached the 12th Army G-2 (intelligence staff officer at division headquarters) I emphasized these prisoners were truly Luxembourgers based on my knowledge of German and their dialect. They obviously were not hardened German soldiers but victims of the occupation forced into service. Their story seemed highly credible.
>
> After the G-2 read my report, he told me he believed the Germans sent these kids to deceive us so we wouldn't move our units to more active areas. He emphasized the

Germans no longer possessed all that kind of spare equipment that they could move into this relatively quiet frontal area.

In reality the troop buildup in the Luxembourg area was only the beginning. Further, greater concentrations of men and equipment were hidden throughout the densely forested areas in eastern Belgian and France. When the attack began on December 16th 1944 it took the allies "entirely" by surprise. Noted factors contributing to the Germans' initial success included: overconfidence, preoccupation with Allied offensive plans, and poor aerial reconnaissance due to bad weather.

I am sure Siegfried's group missed the apology note from headquarters when the Battle of the Bulge began. However, he would be the first to admit things aren't quite as clear, and mistakes are made in the middle of a war. Plus, not every staff level American officer trusted officers who were ex-German patriots. While he never considered filing a complaint, he always felt prejudice existed on some level. Still, Dad wishes he could have done more. Unfortunately, his military protocol afforded him few options.

While not on the frontlines during the major part of the Bulge offensive, Siegfried's 83rd division, nicknamed Thunderbolt, moved around and fought a lot. In early December 1944, they battled in the Hurtgen Forest near Aachen, Germany. Near the end of the Bulge attack, they moved back to Belgium and Luxembourg and helped eliminate the enemy's advance by January 1945.

In late February, the great advance into Germany began as the German army retreated, and abandoned equipment along the route. Many of the German vehicles were painted over with the U.S. star insignia, and used to transport supplies and men. This helped speed the advance. With all these odd, mismatched vehicles in their columns, the 83rd soon became known as the Rag Tag Circus.

Throughout Germany, they liberated British and U.S. prisoners of war, freed concentration and labor camp inmates, and arrested and interrogated local and national Nazi leaders. They crossed the Rhine near Düsseldorf, pursued the enemy through northern German provinces, and reached the Elbe River before any other Allied division.

As they drove into one town, women swarmed toward the column. When Siegfried spoke to them, one woman started screaming, "This man speaks German!" Another explained they were refugees from an abandoned concentration camp.

Today, Siegfried believes it might have been the Bergen-Belsen camp of *The Diary of Anne Frank* fame. It was approximately forty miles from their position. The women were searching for food and supplies, and they told Siegfried many disabled prisoners were still at the camp.

When he saw these desperate, emaciated women in their ragged prison garbs, he couldn't help but become emotionally distraught. His unit was still under orders to advance, so all he could do was reassure them by instructing them to continue away from the front. More settled military units might be able to provide help. Eventually a military government would help.

The image of those women along with others, would haunt my father for the rest of his life. At the time though, he had no idea about the extent of the Holocaust, or its impact on the Jewish and German population, or even his own family. Documents he has passed down to me, in the way of an extensive family record, revealed the following:[1]

- Ferdinand Meinstein born August 29th, 1878 in Zirndorf, died 1942 Auschwitz
- Kaufman Schwetzer born April 25, 1872 in Windsbach, died Jan. 27, 1943 Theresienstadt Concentration Camp
- Hannchen (Meinstein) Schwetzer (wife of Kaufman) born September 12th, 1877 in Oerringer, died with husband Jan. 27th, 1943 Theresienstadt Concentration Camp
- Heinrich (Herman) Meinstein born July 19th, 1882 in Zirndorf died 1942 in Auschwitz[2]
- Hedwig Riesser orn Feb. 23rd 1890 in Zirndorf died 1942 in Auschwitz (note 1)
- Paula Hamburger born June 28th 1872 in Colinberg died in 1943 in Theresienstadt Concentration Camp
- Siegfried Aal born May 10th, 1878 in Egenhausen died in 1942 in Riga Concentration Camp
- Risa Schloss born Nov. 4th, 1888 in Forcheim died in 1942 in Riga Concentration Camp

On April 16th 1945, a week after President Roosevelt's death, the Rag Tag Circus crossed the pontoon Truman Bridge over the formidable Elbe in northwest Germany at the town of Barby. Siegfried's CIC unit apprehended three human torpedoes on a suicide mission to destroy the bridge. During their long advance, they encountered

1 These are all relatives of mine (Ronald S. Meinstein) on my father's side. The records he passed on to me show that our heritage in Zirndorf, Germany can be dated back to the year 1640.

2 Some questions exist about death location. May have been Riga CC, but I went with my dad's hand written note over the family document —Ron

only moderate resistance of mainly small arms fire from a German Volksstrurm, or people's storm troop.

When the futility became apparent, these troops, consisting largely of men forty-five to sixty-five years old, and teenagers from twelve to sixteen, began surrendering. Upon interrogation, they told a fairly consistent story. The road to Berlin, roughly fifty miles away, was intact and lightly guarded. Most of the remaining German resistance had been directed east of Berlin against the Russian advance. This was reported to headquarters, but orders were to remain in position by the Elbe.

Some years later, it became apparent that, this decision near the end of the war, was partially politically motivated. While allies during the war, Russian and American interests over post war land control, and political philosophies had begun. Eventually, this would lead to a break in allegiance, and lead to the "cold war" era. After watching the movie *Patton,* with George C. Scott in the title role, I am sure at least General Patton understood. While constantly criticized for a lack of diplomacy, Patton foresaw the upcoming rivalry, and wasn't afraid to tell the Russians what he thought of them (and it wasn't very nice).

For the most part, this concluded Siegfried's fighting role as the war ended in May 1945. However, he continued to serve in the CIC. As most U.S. troops returned home to hero's welcomes with ticker-tape parades, parties, reunions, and multitudes of grateful women (which led to the baby boom), Siegfried's unit was reassigned to the Munich area. Their job was to hunt, capture, and interrogate German army insurgents, officers, and Nazi leaders.

Although this was a dangerous mission, the strict Allied military rule and attitude of the German people made it tolerable. Surprising to some Americans, the great majority of Germans showed little hostility toward their vanquishers. Acts of insurgency or subversion were relatively rare. Germans were caught in disillusionment, grieving multiple losses, broken families, and a sense of despair over another black mark in their country's history. While the Allied military presence was somewhat unnerving, it helped to reestablish order, as mourning and rebuilding once again began.

One of the first leads for Siegfried's group led to the capture of roughly fifty Hungarian refugees. Many were believed to be members of the insurgent Hungarian government in hiding. In essence, they were alleged to be war criminals, responsible for sending Russian prisoners to the Auschwitz concentration camp, among other charges.

Troop support was concentrated in larger cities. So, it fell to Siegfried and two military truck drivers to transfer the prisoners roughly fifty miles, through semi-mountainous terrain, from Pfarrkirchen, Germany, to Salzburg, Austria. The slow trek over rocky roads took roughly four hours. While Siegfried was following the two troop carrier trucks in his confiscated Opel convertible sedan, a prisoner jumped from a truck and escaped into the tundra. Siegfried regretted he couldn't leave the convoy to chase him down; but they completed the transfer without further incident.

Over the next months, Siegfried's group rounded up many other suspected Nazi criminals. After interrogation, most were sent to Nuremberg, Germany, for the famous trials.

One day, two British officers approached him with a tip. One was Major Hugh Trevor-Roper, a former history professor at the University of Oxford, who was in charge of uncovering the details of Hitler's last days and final demise. He shared with Siegfried the location of former SS Colonel Wilhelm Zander. Zander had been the adjutant to Hitler's personal secretary, Martin Bormann, the head of the Party Chancellery.

Siegfried, along with the two British officers, approached the house where Zander was staying, at three in the morning. The officers watched from a distance as Siegfried knocked on the door. When no one answered, he shouted some pretext in German, which prompted Zander to open the door. Siegfried pinned Zander to the wall, and shoved his fist in his mouth, to prevent him from taking a cyanide capsule. Zander surrendered without a fight, and they recovered a copy of Hitler's last will and testament.

In his 1947 book *The Last Days of Hitler,* Trevor-Roper gave some credit to Siegfried's unit for the raid.

Most captures were not nearly as dramatic, and were aided by a generally helpful German public. Indeed, the last thing most German citizens wanted was more trouble. Many wanted desperately to put the war behind them, and to return to their routine lives.

It was during these tumultuous times, that fate led to the intersection of my mother and fathers' stories.

Maria meets Siegfried

In Reichenberg, a village with five hundred residents, Maria's family rented a house from a widower, who had a daughter about a year older than Maria. It marked a turning point for Maria, who was extremely well received by the landlord and neighbors. This was where she was given her nickname of Mimi and called Mimilein or Mimikin (roughly translated as Mimi loved one) by many.

The landlord, Ludwig Schambock, was a good man, and around 1950, married Maria's mom. When my family visited in the 1960s, he was still working hard in his backyard salvage yard, at eighty years old. The Munich press had recognized him for his service to the community. While I was there, he started up an old wood and metal steam thrasher, which he later dismantled for scrap. I will never forget the deafening noise of driving gears and steam turbine. He let me help stoke the fire, and watched as the smoke rose high above us.

He and my grandmother lived there with my aunt and cousins. Even then, the several old wooden buildings only had cold running water and an outhouse. They warmed water on the stove and hauled it to the tub in the barn. As the guest of honor, I would take a bath first, followed by my cousins.

Shortly after my bath, as I walked toward the house a pigeon pooped on my head. All I could think to say to my cousins in my limited German was, "It is raining." We all laughed for several minutes. What I remember most was the love and sense of family, which I find even more amazing in light of my mom's difficult youth.

Mimi was about nineteen when they moved. One of her first needs was a closer job. However, she quickly found a secretarial job at the air force training school, about an hour away by bicycle—roughly a dozen miles. She lived in the women's barracks during the week, and spent weekends at home.

One of her duties brought home the Nazi regime's evilness. Adjacent to the training facility was a small subcamp of the infamous Mauthausen concentration camp, which was approximately sixty miles away in Austria. The inmates of this subcamp were mainly political prisoners. The guards gathered meat and vegetables for the camp at the local farms. Mimi was ordered to accompany the horse-drawn wagon, because she spoke the local dialect.

The prisoners wore ragged clothing, and suffered from malnutrition. It was obvious the staff was plundering the farm supplies. One day as the wagon passed by, she tossed some produce over the fence to the starving inmates as covertly as she could. Unfortunately, a guard caught her and severely reprimanded her. However, she was allowed to keep her secretarial job, and was never again forced to return to the camp.

Other than the concentration camp duty, she enjoyed her duties at the school. However, the Allied bombers overhead frequently distracted her near the end of the war. The family's decision to move to a less populated area had proven to be a good one. And thankfully, the training school wasn't a major military target.

One weekend, though, an Allied plane flew low over the countryside near the war's end, while she was riding her bicycle. She was terrified because she knew people who had been killed in nearby bombings, and strafing attacks.

Mimi dropped her bicycle and jumped into a roadside ditch. The plane circled back, and made another pass significantly lower and directly at Mimi. Mimi peeped up and could see the pilots smiling. The plane seemed to wave its wings as it pulled away. As Mimi dusted off her blouse and skirt, she smiled at the apparent military-style flirtation.

Dating wasn't a big part of her youth. Young women in Germany lacked opportunities at that time, with most adult males involved with the war. Things were too serious, and she didn't want to jeopardize her job by getting a reputation. She did occasionally attend social engagements with air force officers.

About two weeks before the war ended, the air force training school was decommissioned, and the employees were released. Mimi packed her belongings and returned home. While she liked her job, she loved spending more time in tranquil little Reichenberg. Forests and farms nearby beckoned, and the Rott River was about ten minutes away.

It was there where she met Jacqueline Nanay, a Hungarian refugee who became her best friend. Jackie, as Mimi called her, was well educated and spoke French, in addition to Hungarian and German. She lived with her family in a small farmhouse nearby, and had access to horses. Mimi, while a little afraid at first, finally mounted a horse and rode through the forests with Jacky. They spent endless hours visiting, walking, and talking.

One Saturday afternoon, Jackie and Mimi decided to take a long walk to an old bridge that both of them had only seen from a distance. Amid the beautiful pastoral setting, they ate bag lunches, and talked about anything and everything, as girls tend to do. Before they realized it, night fell.

Still chatting with no sense of urgency, they headed back through the town of Pfarrkirchen. Mimi commented on how quiet, peaceful, and dark the town was. Jackie turned to Mimi and said, "Oh, it is curfew!"

This didn't mean much to Mimi, because she was never out after dark except in their garden. As she was thinking how spooky the town seemed, a loud American jeep pulled up beside them and a soldier yelled at them to halt. He turned to talk to a fellow soldier in English, and then asked the women in surprisingly fluent German, "Where do you think you are going? Don't you know that nobody is allowed out after eight o'clock?"

The officer—my future father—noticed these young women looked innocent and scared. They had no identification, which wasn't unusual after the war. He noted their names and addresses, and ordered them to hurry home, and to report to his office in the former city hall on Monday.

I once asked my dad about his first impressions of Mimi during that first encounter. First, she was pretty, or as he put it, "She made a good impression." Second, he was surprised by how scared she appeared. To his way of thinking, he was merely enforcing the curfew, and didn't mean to seem threatening. Her lips trembled as her body shook. Siegfried later discovered this condition was chronic, and occurred whenever Mimi was upset. It took her years, and much reassurance from Siegfried and others, to overcome much of her physical and mental trauma.

After the jeep drove off, the two women walked home silently into the darkness. At the point where they had to separate, they shared a quick goodbye. Jackie descended a small forest road on the other side of the Rott River, while Mimi scampered up the hill. As Mimi approached the house, she noticed the lights were off, further increasing her anxiety.

That Sunday seemed longer than any other Mimi could remember. Sleep eluded her for most of the night. Jackie reported as instructed at ten in the morning with her father, and returned home in her father's care, with strict instructions. Mimi had to languish four additional hours. Finally, two o'clock arrived, and Mimi walked into the Counter Intelligence headquarters, alone and scared.

First Lieutenant Meinstein politely asked Mimi to take a seat in perfect German. He asked if she had any connections with the Nazi Party, and about her employment history. Knowing my dad, he was confirming what he had already researched about her.

"Can you cook?" he asked.

"Yes, a little," she said.

"Can you prepare a duck dinner with red cabbage?"

She shook her head no.

"Do you know anyone who could prepare such a dinner?"

She immediately mentioned that her mother was the best cook she knew. He offered her a job, cleaning and cooking at their officers' house.

She felt like she had little choice, so she agreed to report for duty in two days, and to tell nobody except for her mother.

The Counter Intelligence Corps had confiscated a large, nice three-bedroom home on top of a hill to house the four officers. She didn't know the owners, as they were sophisticated, and didn't associate with most of Reichenberg's poorer inhabitants.

Mimi shook as she arrived at the elegant house, and walked through the beautiful, fenced-in garden. As instructed, she had brought nothing with her. She tentatively rang the doorbell, and an American officer opened the door and motioned her into the living room.

She never imagined she would ever step foot in this house! It was just as she had pictured, full of ornate trinkets and beautiful furniture. The Americans obviously had taken fairly good care of it. The first lieutenant who hired her walked in comfortably dressed, instead of in uniform. He gave her a tour, and instructions for cooking and cleaning.

Just as Mimi started to relax a little, the officer broke the news that she had to live in the house, because of the sensitive nature of their mission. She was not to communicate with anyone about anything that went on. Mimi pushed back by saying she had to tell her mother. He responded that he would take care of that.

Mimi got into her routine, and slept on the couch. Four officers were living there, including Siegfried, who was the boss. They all treated her with respect, and she noticed Siegfried seemed to be fond of her. He seemed to look at her with more than just the appreciation of a grateful employer? He was beginning to trust her, and allow her to talk to her mom on occasion, though never away from the house.

When her mom arrived that first Sunday, they marveled at the house together. The kitchen was set up different from her mother's, but they adapted. Along with everything else, the stove was superior to any they had ever seen. Their duck dinner came out perfectly. Everyone came into the kitchen to compliment them. Her mama was paid well, but Mimi still couldn't go home.

Siegfried explained he preferred that his acquaintances call him Sidney. Later, she discovered this was his way of rebelling against one of Hitler's favorite operas, *Siegfried* by Richard Wagner. He didn't want any connection to Hitler, and especially didn't want Germans to call him Siegfried. As I grew up, Mom would call him Sid when we were alone. In fact, my middle name is Sidney. It would have been my first name, but mom won that discussion.

One evening, about a week after the duck dinner, the priest and some parishioners from the Catholic Church in Pfarrkirchen came to the house. They said, not only were Mimi's mom and landlord concerned about her living in the house, but also the entire population of Reichenberg. The Americans said they appreciated the concern, and the respectful way it was delivered.

After a short discussion, they agreed Mimi could go home at night, if she promised to not discuss anything she saw or heard at the house with anybody. Mimi promised, and the group said a prayer. The priest shook everyone's hands, and thanked the officers for their understanding and compassion.

Mimi collected her things and walked out with the church folks. Other townspeople waiting just outside the property, shook Mimi's hand and hugged her. Mimi hadn't realized how loved she was by so many people! After that, she felt so much freer.

Of course, even though she was always treated well, it felt a bit awkward, as a pretty young woman, alone in a house full of young men. Sidney, however, had assumed the role of protector, and was even somewhat possessive of her. She could tell he sincerely liked her, and never fought his possessiveness. Her feelings for him grew over time.

Food was never a problem for Mimi and the Americans. They grew an abundant supply of vegetables in the garden, raised chickens, and acquired meats and supplies from local farmers. Occasionally, when approved, her mom would show up to help with a meal. However, they missed candy and sweet treats.

One evening, a jeep drove up as Mimi, her mother, and stepfather were talking after dinner in their cozy home. Guess who? It was Sidney, with a rather large bag of candies, chocolates, and other sweet treats. The four of them sat down, and shared coffee and much more.

Mimi was quick to notice his demeanor was completely different from his usual persona of the confident, decisive American officer. He was cordial, soft spoken, and empathetic. Mimi's family immediately liked him, and enjoyed their conversation. Even though Sidney was obviously highly educated, he didn't make them feel inferior. The reality of their common roots, love for what Germany should have been, and desire for peace created a greater bond.

As it became clear to residents that, Sidney's counter intelligence mission was finding high-ranking Nazis and war criminals, information came easier. Their group had established an effective network, which frequently led to leads. The few German Jews were particularly helpful. The group made a number of arrests, and sent prisoners for further processing.

The increased trust between Sidney and Mimi afforded more freedom. Mimi's workload lessened as Sidney hired more women to help at the house. This freed her up to spend a lot of time in the garden and to visit with friends. During the summer, she occasionally took a couple of little neighbor children, Christa and Irmgard, swimming in the Rott River. She no longer saw Jackie very often, except at the swimming area. They had grown apart after their traumatic interviews.

One day, while in the office, an officer asked Mimi to type a report, and she noticed her name. While she had learned a little spoken English, she had no idea what the report said. Upset, she asked what she had just typed. The officer told her it was nothing and tore up the report.

It actually was a test to see if Mimi could accurately type without understanding. After that, she typed for the unit, because the men were getting complaints about their handwritten reports. Mimi was thrilled, and felt useful. From then on, the only person complaining about their bad handwriting was Mimi. She no longer worked in the house, but occasionally helped take notes at interviews.

A few months later, Sidney had to attend a sectional meeting in Passau, and invited Mimi along. By now, she had grown to love spending time with Sidney. Also, this would be a rare adventure!

Sidney's boss, the colonel in charge of the Bavarian region, instantly liked Mimi and introduced her to his wife, who had recently joined him from the States. They occupied a stately home in Passau.

Mimi spoke a little English, and the colonel's wife spoke a little German. They hit it off. Mimi was surprised that, other officers had brought German girlfriends to the meetings. While the men spent the days in meetings, the women visited with each other. In the evenings, the men and women would unite for sumptuous dinners. Mimi was now officially known as Sidney's girl.

For one of the first times in Mimi's life, she had nothing to worry about. Sidney ensured that her family always had good food, and she spent most of her spare time with him.

During the next year, Mimi accompanied Sidney when he was transferred to the town of Deggendorf on the Danube River, and later to Grafenau outside of the Bavarian Forest. While Mimi still helped with reports, it was not nearly a full-time job. She had a lot of time to make friends in town, and with co-workers. She also loved exploring the new areas. Young and in love, she and Sidney spent their time together in the evenings.

Even though Sidney's job was serious, the country's mood had shifted. For the most part, grief was dissipating, with healing underway. Although under occupation, most Germans were more concerned with resuming their lives, and recovering what they could of the Germany they remembered.

Mimi and Sidney enjoyed going out into the community with a fair amount of freedom. They also attended military functions, which included social affairs. One even featured a boat party on the Danube. For a young lady with such a traumatic upbringing, all of the fun and freedom felt overwhelming.

One day, Sidney brought Mimi a present—a lovely Irish setter puppy. Mimi named it Otta, and took her everywhere. Otta loved to sleep in her bed and stretch out like a person.

Everything felt perfect, and Sidney and Mimi talked about marriage. Outside of work, they enjoyed nice dinners, and a few parties with the officers and their wives or girlfriends.

One of the women Sidney had hired was a former Hungarian schoolteacher, who he considered sharp. She spoke excellent English and gave English lessons to Mimi, who was very fond of her.

Sidney had given his family the good news about Mimi. When he got his six-week furlough, he gave Mimi his class ring, with a promise to return. She spent time with her family while he visited his parents in America.

Maria Liegl and Siegfried Meinstein with Otta in Germany in 1947.

Sidney couldn't wait an entire six weeks and returned to Germany after just four. After surprising Mimi with his early return, and the mandatory hugs and kisses in front of her home, he proposed. He didn't bend down on one knee, and/or offer an engagement ring. That came later. Dad has always been a first things first kind of guy. It didn't matter to Mimi; she was thrilled! To her this was like the ending of *Cinderella*, with her in the title role.

Sidney soon retired from active service, but worked as a civilian in a similar capacity for the War Department—for better pay and less stress.

When men from Sidney's unit in the Bavarian Forest heard about the wedding, they helped plan it. One man from the Simbach area, about fifteen miles from Mimi's home, did most of the work, such as hiring a pastry chef, known for delicious cakes and pastries. He also pilfered the unit's cigarette rations, for informants, to arrange other food and an orchestra. While food was scarce, cigarettes were even scarcer. Isn't addiction wonderful?

On January 24, 1948, they were married in a beautiful Catholic Church in Simbach am Inn, a small town in the Rottal-Inn district of Bavaria. Mimi's mother, stepfather, neighbors, and Sidney's military buddies attended. From their pictures, you couldn't tell the wedding occurred so soon after the war, except for the uniforms. I don't think I ever saw my mom with a broader smile, except maybe in pictures, where she was holding me as a baby.

Two weeks later, they embarked on a grand honeymoon that Sidney had planned. From Munich, they took the train to Rome, and stayed in the best, relatively undamaged, hotel they could find. They were treated like royalty by the Italians, who were grateful to American soldiers. A restaurant even gave their dog, Otta, spaghetti. Otta didn't know how to eat the noodles, but she eventually tossed them in the air and caught them in her mouth. Needless to say, this became an instant attraction for the restaurant.

After Rome, they enjoyed Naples and Capri without many tourists. Much of the devastation hadn't been repaired, but the locals were eager to please the happy honeymooners. People probably were eager to find a reason to celebrate.

They had decided to move near Sidney's family in America. Sidney made it sound like such an adventure, and a better place to live. He assured Mimi that, they would return as often as possible (and we did). Still, for Mimi this was one of the most difficult moves ever. While her memories were very mixed, it was her family and friends who she would deeply miss. Many years later she shared with me that, she never knew how much leaving must have affected her mom until she had me. Still, she knew they had made the best decision.

After their two-week honeymoon, they cruised to New York on the *Vulcania* ocean liner. They traveled second class with Otta, and docked in about ten days.

Mimi and Sidney were surprised to stumble upon a big parade when they arrived. It felt like a homecoming celebration, in their honor. A crowd formed to admire Otta, who happened to be wearing a cute green collar and leash. You guessed it. Everyone thought their red-haired Irish setter was part of the St. Patrick's Day festivities!

A few days later, they took the train to Chicago, where Sidney's mother had rented a small apartment for them, despite the severe housing shortage after the war. Their new home was close to his parents, who immediately liked Mimi, and were excited to introduce her to family and friends.

Siegfried and Maria Meinstein with Otta on their honeymoon in Italy in February 1948.

Mimi adapted to American life well, as her English was quite passable by then. She quickly got a job on State Street, downtown at Mandel Brothers, a multistory department store, similar to Marshall Field's or Macy's. She used the streetcar every day for transportation.

Sidney, while always good to Mimi, didn't fare as well. He may have suffered from what we now call post-traumatic stress disorder. He did find a job as a control chemist for a steel mill. However, he sunk into a depression when his parents died within a month of each other in 1954. One day he just stopped his car in the middle of a major Chicago street. Another car hit his car. He suffered numerous broken bones and lost teeth. He was hospitalized, and treated for physical and psychiatric disorders for over six months. Thanks to Mimi's devoted care and his doctors, he consistently improved. After his release, he was still grieving the loss of his parents, but in general had a positive attitude.

Siegfried got a good job with Witco Chemical Company in Chicago. He worked there for three decades, until he retired in 1985. Six years into their marriage, I showed up.

World War II served as the backdrop for many other equally unlikely romantic stories, which leads to our next saga of Crystal's parents, Mary Jane and Jim Carlson.

Siegfried Meinstein carried this photo of his wife and son, Maria and Ron, in his wallet for at least fifty-eight years.

During Ron Meinstein's first visit to Germany in 1954, his stepfather, Ludwig Schambock held him while his grandmother, Maria Liegl closely watched at their home in Reichenberg, Germany.

III

Jim and Mary Jane

Crystal

It was 1955. Mary Jane Carlson, 30 years old, and the other new mothers in the large Chicago hospital ward heard people running down the hall.

"Someone must be really sick," they whispered.

Mom had just given birth to me, a healthy eight-pound baby girl, who she named Crystal Ann. She got to pick the name that time because Dad had named my older brother, their nineteen-month-old son, Lawrence Wayne. Mom would have preferred Jeffrey.

Within seconds, a herd of doctors and nurses stampeded in and surrounded Mom's bed.

"What's the matter?" she asked, looking from one anxious face to another.

"You have a severe case of pernicious anemia," said the doctor who had delivered me. "We think you are going to die. Most people don't survive this."

The other mothers in the ward looked upset, afraid they would be next to get bad news, but Mom was not upset.

"I have two babies to take care of," she said with a determined expression. "This is no time to die."

To the surprise and relief of the doctors, she survived the anemia, and was able to take care of Larry and me. She wasn't allowed to nurse me even though she wanted to, because of the anemia. Several months later, Mom and Dad moved with their two babies into a one-story, white-frame, two-bedroom house, on Yale Avenue in Roseland, a neighborhood on the south side of Chicago. Later, when I was ten, we would move into the brick house in Dolton, Illinois, a few miles farther south. And another ten years later, my parents were still faring well, when I fell in love with Ron at Bradley University, about one hundred fifty miles away in Peoria, Illinois.

When Ron met Mom and Dad in 1975, he instantly liked them. They were cordial, well-mannered, and conservative. While Ron believed Mom liked him, Dad took a while to warm up. After all, Ron was dating his daughter, and no one ever would be good enough. As a father of three daughters, Ron understands that now. He recognized the impact of a strict upbringing, centered on family, typical of many who had grown up during the Great Depression. Raised by parents with similar values, Ron had instant respect for them.

Ron was a fan of all the mother-in-law jokes, so prevalent in the seventies. However, he couldn't contribute to those, even with his sense of humor, which our daughters classify as corny and old fashioned. Mom was one of the sweetest, most caring souls he had ever known. If someone mistreated Mom, she wouldn't get angry. Instead she would somehow defend them. As she explained, that person must be coping with a difficult experience, or had endured a rough life.

When Ron and I encountered the typical newlywed communication tiffs, I would ask Mom for advice. Although Ron didn't know how Mom had advised me, he would find me much calmer, perhaps apologetic, and ready to resolve our differences. Mom used to warn us that marriage wasn't easy and demanded constant work, but it was worth the effort.

One day when Ron wasn't in a great mood, he critiqued Mom's chili. Even though he realized she had cooked a nice dinner for us, he told her it tasted like tomato soup with hamburger and beans. This was before he learned my dad's history of ulcers. Early in their marriage, my mom realized she couldn't add many typical spices to her cooking. He felt mean as the words spilled out.

Mom's response? "I have always wanted to be a better cook, and I would appreciate any help you could give me."

Although Ron regretted his comment, of course, he did end up helping her with some recipes, and cooked for my parents as often as possible.

Dad has always been available for us with wise counsel, even when unsolicited. He was quick to give us the conservative point of view on any venture we were planning. Skiing, rock climbing, and football were too dangerous, for example.

Of course, Dad always took my side during my disagreements with Ron. Ron might not have gotten along as well with Dad if he hadn't respected my father's position. He understood Dad wasn't greedy or self-centered; he was simply a caring father trying to protect us.

We truly believed Mom and Dad were meant to be together. This is their story, highlighting how a war and an unlikely set of circumstances led to their meeting, courtship mostly by mail, and eventual marriage.

Mary Jane

Mary Jane Johnson was born in April 1925 to Marian Elizabeth (McCune) Johnson and Harold Johnson in Kenosha, Wisconsin. Mom was the first child of the family's fourth generation to reside in the white colonial two-story house, that had remained in the family for ninety years. It was in a nice neighborhood, of single-family homes, with immigrant families and Americans. Grandma's father was Irish, and this was an influence on the household. There was a small front yard, and a large back yard with a barn.

Mom and her parents lived there with her grandfather and great aunt, called Nonny John, who owned it. Grandma Marian moved in with her father when she was twelve years old, after her parents divorced. I remember her wearing flowered housedresses and aprons, with her dark gray hair parted in the middle and pinned into a bun. She was always cooking, cleaning, crocheting or sewing.

Mom was named after her wealthy relatives, Aunt Mary and Aunt Jane. Grandma and Grandpa wrongly believed they would be generous with their namesake. While Mom understood her parent's motives, she was disappointed by her lack of a middle name.

Around the corner lived her father's mother, Great Grandma Frieda Johnson, who emigrated from Denmark on a ship when she was twelve. I remember her long white braided hair wrapped around her head, her flowered housedresses covered by aprons, and her dark manly shoes. On a large black stove, she baked cookies, cakes, and pies that Mom and I savored. I grew up eating her ebelskivers, a Danish type of doughnut hole fried in a specialized cast-iron pan. She rolled the hot orbs in confectioners' sugar or cinnamon and sugar. Great Grandma gave the pan to Grandma Marian, who passed it on to Aunt Joann and then to Mom. We use the pan in our house, to make ebelskivers for our girls and our grandchildren.

During the Wisconsin autumns, the apple tree in Great Grandma Frieda's backyard meant pies and applesauce, a tradition which Mom wove into her marriage. My dad bought two bushels of Jonathan apples from an orchard every fall, and Jeannette, Larry, and I peeled them after school and on weekends. We enlisted help from friends, beckoned by the fragrance of apple pie baking, and applesauce bubbling on the stove. Mom ensured her assistants received some applesauce and a slice of pie, either two-crusted or apple crumb. Mom's pies, such as lemon meringue, rhubarb custard, butterscotch meringue and pecan, were heavenly.

Great Grandma Frieda lived with her daughter, Mom's Aunt Alice, who resembled a pristine china doll. Aunt Alice, Great Grandma Johnson, and all the relatives helped raise Mom. For six years, Mom, nicknamed Snooky, was the lone child in a house of opinionated relatives. Mom became easygoing and cooperative, because she had to be a diplomat to survive. Growing up with numerous authority figures, she learned it's easier to avoid conflict than resolve it. She would say, "I'd rather switch than fight." Her peacemaking skills helped forge many friendships.

Elections, though, crushed any diplomacy. Half of Mom's family was made up of Republicans, and the other half Democrats. Elections brewed fiery arguments, but the only unpardonable offence was not voting. Arguments broke out over dinner, sometimes escalating until someone retreated from the table.

Ron once teased Mom about not wanting to vote for any of the candidates. He swears, the color drained from her face, with a scathing look of disappointment.

"Did you know voting is not only a right, but a responsibility?" she asked.

Ron loves to tease, but he quickly decided that wasn't a good time, or subject. He had to agree, and told her he respected her passion for our country.

Emotion in Mom's family was not limited to elections. Relatives also fled the table when Grandma or Grandpa disciplined her. Ron and I can't imagine her doing anything worthy of a swat at the table.

As a little girl, Mom adored her black cocker spaniel. His death, during her childhood unleashed so much sorrow that, she never wanted another pet, even as she raised us. One of my happiest memories was when, after three years of marriage, Ron and I adopted two stray cats, Peter and Samantha, my first pets.

Grandma Marian collected animals, from chickens, ducks, and geese to cats, dogs, and parrots. Mom's younger siblings, Aunt Joann, Aunt Helen, and Uncle Cliff, became attached to a goose that followed them around like a puppy. Many tears fell the evening the pet goose ended up on the dinner menu.

Grandma Marian's aunt, known as Nonny John, suffered from *tuberculosis,* and was confined to her upstairs bedroom. Nonny was a veracious reader and very knowledgeable. Mom became very close with her as they discussed books, and tackled Mom's homework together, because Grandma Marian was busy with housework, cooking, and nursing the older relatives.

When Mom was three, she welcomed a baby brother, but his life was clipped short. Mom doesn't remember much beyond visiting his grave at the cemetery. Three years later, a sister, Aunt Joann, was born. As they grew, it became apparent that while Mom was skilled at household chores such as ironing and cooking, she was not a quick learner, unlike her sister. Mom's lack of coordination contributed to her difficulties. So even though Mom was six years older, she didn't do chores as often as Aunt Joann.

As a child, Mom loved to ice- and roller-skate. Weather permitting, she even roller-skated several blocks to school. During the winter, she ice-skated at a nearby pond as often as possible. She also loved to dance, and took ballet classes until the day she fell and broke her leg while showing her mom what she had learned. Although her leg quickly healed, it marked the beginning of unfortunate health problems, that seemed to plague her the rest of her life.

Mom had to wear an eyepatch over a lazy eye for a year during elementary school. Of course, it was embarrassing, and classmates made fun of her. It made it difficult to read and exercise.

Living by Lake Michigan meant frigid, wet, snowy winters, falls, and springs. Even in the summer, it rarely exceeded 80 degrees. Mom and Aunt Joann got sick easily, and Aunt Joann had asthma. Every winter, Mom suffered from bronchitis, and coughed, and coughed and coughed.

Children and adults truly suffered before penicillin, or other antibiotics were standard treatment.

Mom was twelve when her youngest sister, Aunt Helen, was born; and about two years later brought the only surviving boy, Uncle Clifford.

Mary Jane Johnson, 3rd from the left, with her siblings, Cliff, Joann and Helen, around 1943.

Mom always said Grandma Marian raised two families: she and Aunt Joann first, and later Aunt Helen and Uncle Cliff. Mom's father, Grandpa Harold Johnson, died when he was fifty-nine after struggling with heart problems for years. So, Grandma became a single mother to the younger children, and not as strict.

Grandpa was ten years older than Grandma Marian. He died when I was a baby. They spent only one year alone in the house without children, or relatives during their entire marriage. Mom said they were very happy together. Life was hard, but they worked at things together. On Saturday nights, they often played cards with Great Grandma Frieda. With all of the laughing and joking, it was obvious they cherished each other. One of Grandma Marian's sayings was, "Isn't love grand?"

Indeed, it was for her and Grandpa.

Grandpa, who was smart and well read, served as a soldier in World War I. After the war, he worked for the automobile industry, which laid off the workers for two months during the summer. This caused a hardship on the family, and Grandpa would do what he could to make money during that stretch.

Regardless, Mom adored her father. She was rarely disobedient, and his mere look of disapproval could make her cry.

During the Depression, Grandpa stood all day in line with other men for a bag of flour or sugar. Everyone nurtured a victory garden during the war. During the Depression, it was just called a garden. Grandma Marian also grew raspberries and vegetables, along with the chickens, ducks and geese.

Mom said people would move out of their houses in the middle of the night during the Depression, when they couldn't pay the mortgage or rent. They would end up in another house a few blocks away. It was an uncertain time, with people coming and going.

Grandma and Grandpa were known for their generosity, and considered Christianity to be a way of life. People called Grandma, or dropped by when they were in trouble. She was always baking and cooking for neighbors and friends as well, stretching food as far as she could. Mom grew to hate the sight of Spam. Sugar was sparse, so they used molasses or honey for baked goods. Everyone bartered.

Several older family members in Mom's household struggled with terrible drinking problems, which ruined many holidays. A call would come in that one of them was drunk somewhere, and Grandpa Harold would have to go fetch him, and sober him up. This caused arguments and conflict, of course, which pitted Mom against drunkenness. She knew how it could hurt the family. Her Great Uncle Freddy and Great Aunt Ethel met at a bar, and they drank until they became what Daddy called "religious fanatics."

When I was young, my dad would tease Mom and say, he liked it better when they were drinking. When we visited at Aunt Joann's house, we formed a prayer circle with Great Aunt Ethel, and Great Uncle Freddy, and our whole family. As children, we didn't understand why we were doing this. Occasionally, Great Aunt Ethel would stop talking. This was confusing, until Mom explained she was having mini strokes. We thought she might be going into a trance.

Mom's great aunt, Nonny John, paid Mom's tuition for Carroll College, in Wisconsin, for the year of 1943. Mom wanted to continue, but felt guilty because her sisters and brother, wouldn't have the same opportunity. College was hard, but she loved it. She didn't like her roommate, and ended up with her own room. As a sorority member, Mom developed many friendships and had fun. In fact, she kept in touch with her sorority sisters for decades. Later in life, she wished she could have majored in home economics, or library science, and gotten her degree.

At college, Mom suffered from debilitating headaches and hallucinations. She told us a man would appear in her room and talk to her. One day, she felt an explosion in her head, and the headaches and visions stopped. The doctors that took care of her in the future could not figure out what happened to her. Later in life, in her forties, she faced balance problems. Some of her doctors believed the equilibrium problems stemmed from those headaches.

World War II coincided with her college year. After she returned home, she worked in a factory, cranking out metal screws for the war effort. Even though the work was exhausting and boring, she didn't complain. Mom was glad she could help her family, and her country while saving money.

For recreation, Mom joined the United Service Organizations (USO) in Kenosha, met servicemen, and enjoyed the music and dancing. In fact, Mom wrote many servicemen who went overseas. Grandma Marian joked that she was supporting the post office. Mom hoped they would write back, but most didn't. Her dates were casual, but one local young man did propose marriage. However, Mom turned him down as gently as possible, leaving open the opportunity for her to meet Dad.

NEEDLEWORK

As long as Ron has known me, my passion has been needlework. While he has acquired some understanding of knitting, crocheting, and quilting over the years, he knows more than he wants to about redwork embroidery and candlewicking.

Ron realizes the obvious therapeutic aspect of my cloth-based arts. I am never more peaceful than sitting on the couch with a piece of fabric, yarn, or another needle-and-thread project. The battle of cats trying to sit in my lap or play with my thread, scissors, yarn, and pins only adds to the serenity.

Quilting is my favorite, which I do by hand. Ron believes the longarm quilting machines of today are jealous of my tiny, meticulously placed stitches.

Ron never had to wonder where my love of needlecrafts originated. When he met me, Mom was teaching quilting classes in our Dolton home, around the kitchen table. One time he came for dinner, I told him to hurry up and finish eating so we could clear the table. The quilting ladies, who already knew about Ron and me, were coming soon!

Quilting is often passed down from generation to generation. We called my mom's house in Cincinnati the quilt house, because most of the rooms, and the beds, displayed quilts. Our house is similar, with quilted wall hangings in the living room, dining room, large bathroom, and some of the bedrooms. I change them seasonally and pull out special ones for fall, Christmas, and Easter.

Our three daughters appreciate the quilt crafts my mom and I have made for them. Michelle made a small wall hanging for a class in school, but otherwise the girls don't seem interested in quilting. I believe at least one of them will make quilts someday, though. Ron likes the wall and bed quilts, and even admires the quilting clothing that my mom and I have made.

Until we began this book, though, he never understood the depth of the preoccupation in the Carlson/Johnson family line. Grandma Marian, Aunt Alice, and the other aunts, and Great Grandma Frieda did needle arts. As a young child, I watched Grandma Marian crochet with thread to craft beautiful tablecloths, bedspreads, and doilies. She knitted clothing, crafted handmade quilts, and embroidered tablecloths, pillowcases, quilt blocks, and other items. She taught Mom to stitch, embroider, knit, and quilt.

Great Grandma Frieda crocheted, knitted, embroidered, and quilted, even embroidering into her nineties. Racine Nonny, Mom's great aunt, who lived in Racine, Wisconsin, also embroidered and quilted. Grandma Marian and Racine Nonny sometimes pieced the blocks together with the sewing machine, but mostly they hand pieced and hand quilted.

Grandma Marian gathered her friends weekly for what they called the Koffee Klatch. Mom remembers, at a very early age, sitting under the quilt they were working on, and listening to their stories and discussions of the day's events. Quilting and needle arts brought women together, to support each, and discuss the issues of the day.

Mom loved listening to the day's social networking from her little quilt fort. But one day at her cousin Buddy's house, when they were both five, Buddy lured her out of her cozy fort. He led her to the garage, where his father had left a gallon of bright red paint temptingly open, where little hands could reach it.

Buddy's dad's car, as most cars of that period, was the most boring shade of black. Surely, a bright red paint job would be a great surprise for the family!

A surprise, yes, but not so great.

They were about halfway finished when Grandma Marian and Buddy's mother finally started wondering where the kids were.

Soon the quilting ladies were springing up when they heard Grandma scream. Wasting no time to admire the artwork, they grabbed rags from the garage and saved the car by wiping the paint off before it completely dried.

Mom and Buddy were never alone again until adulthood. Mom wasn't usually naughty, but she just couldn't resist the color red. Dad ended up buying a number of red cars for our family because of Mom.

The lure of needlework was also compelling for Mom. With her eventual goal of joining her mom and other relatives in their sewing projects, she took sewing classes in junior high school. She disliked the teachers, who ripped out many of the stitches in everything she tried to make; so, she learned from Grandma Marian instead.

At nine years old, Mom and her best friend, Roberta Walker, pieced quilts together on her front porch. Some of these pieces lasted throughout my childhood. When I was in high school, Mom found an embroidered quilt top she had made as a child, and we ended up basting it and hand quilting it together. This experience was very special to me because, I could imagine my mom embroidering this top as a child; and now we were making it into an heirloom quilt.

Mom made clothes for herself, Jeannette and me, and hand-sewed skirts and dresses, when she couldn't use the sewing machine anymore. And as previously stated, she crafted my beautiful lace and beaded wedding dress and train, a work of art and love. Mom not only made quilts and wall hangings, but also an entire wardrobe for herself, plus jackets, coats, vests, and pillows for friends and family. Ron has photographed many of Mom's quilts, wall hangings, and quilted clothing.

When I was in high school, Mom placed an ad in the newspaper to start a quilting group, which ended up meeting for about twenty years. With encouragement from those members and her quilting students, she started a quilt guild in South Holland, Illinois, which still meets today, with more than a hundred members. It's not surprising that Mom became known as the Quilting Lady of Dolton. After Dad retired, they moved in 1989 to Cincinnati, where in some circles, she became the Quilting Lady of Cincinnati.

I learned to quilt in high school, and have since learned design, fabric selection, and basting. I frequently basted quilts together with mom on the living room floor, and hand quilted parts of Mom's quilts. I learned to embroider and sew by hand when I was four. Along with Jeannette, the three of us had our own needlecraft circle.

I knit, crochet with yarn and thread, sew clothes for myself, our girls, and our granddaughters. I refuse to mend Ron's socks, but I have mended his pants. I have taught needlecrafts, and lectured about quilting. Jeannette embroiders, does blackwork, counted cross-stitch, and more crafts.

When I go to a quilt show or work on the baby quilts for my grandchildren, I remember spending time with Mom looking at quilts, and making needlecraft projects. I know that mom is proud of Jeannette and me as we continue to do needlecrafts.

Mary Jane Carlson stands by her "Jesus with the Lambs" quilt that she crafted and donated to hang in the Anderson Hills United Methodist Church in Cincinnati, Ohio, in 2003.

My daughters are very grateful for the handmade gifts they received from my mom, and from Jeannette and me. Sometimes, when I show my girls what I am working on they will say, "Granny would love that, mom." They display my wall hangings in their homes. We have quilted wall hangings of varying sizes displayed in our house, just like Mom had in her house.

I designed and created this quilt "I Want to Go to Tahiti with Ron" to celebrate our 20th wedding anniversary in 1999. It is embroidered, reversed appliqued with a Tahitian design and quilted by hand.

I have my grandmother Marian's green sewing basket on my dresser and my sewing box, thread, scissors, needles, pins, etc. can be seen in our living room quite often. My quilts have been shown in quilt shows in four states, and I have taught quilting, counted cross stitch, embroidery, crocheting, knitting and other crafts over the years. I portray a Civil War lady talking about Harriet Beecher Stowe, her life and her works, and show my redwork embroidered quilt about her at libraries, churches and other places. My mom did her Quilting through the Bible Program for over 20 years, and I am following in her footsteps as a speaker, teacher and quilter.

This round table mandala quilt "The Butterfly Quilt" was made to celebrate our 40th wedding anniversary in 2018. It has 18 attached butterflies. It is embroidered, appliqued, beaded, and quilted by hand.

Childhood in Chicago

My father's mother, Dorothy Davidson, grew up in a farm near Neoga, a small town in southern Illinois. Apparently, Neoga means deer among the Kickapoo people (an Algonquian speaking Native American and indigenous Mexican tribe).

Grandma Carlson's (Dorothy's) parents were Americans from English ancestors. Grandma, who didn't savor farm life, had four sisters and five brothers. While her brothers played musical instruments and learned to become barbers like their father, she and her sisters were relegated to cooking and cleaning.

When Grandma was little, they had a Billy goat that she dearly loved. When the goat died, her siblings and friends held a funeral and parade for him. They carried the flag and sang patriotic songs. Grandma warned me not to get a Billy goat, to protect my heart from getting attached. She stilled missed her goat even decades later!

Her father worked sometimes as a traveling salesman, and brought home odd things, such as a baby alligator that they sequestered in the basement tub. Her mother threw a fit and banished it.

As she grew older, Grandma and her sister, Anne, longed to be independent. One of the few acceptable careers for women back then was a secretary, so they went to stenography school to learn typing and shorthand.

As a young woman, Grandma Dorothy fed her adventurous side. She and Anne traveled out West from one big city to the next, working as stenographers. They enjoyed exploring the area, when they weren't working, until they wanted to move again. In Salt Lake City, Utah, Grandma married a Mormon man. The Mormon relatives were not receptive of the marriage, so after a year, Grandma divorced him, and moved back to Chicago for the rest of her life.

Dad's father, Walfred Otto Carlson, was the only child born in America in a large immigrant Swedish family. Grandpa Carlson grew up in Hobart, Indiana, which was almost a Chicago suburb, close to the Illinois border. He eventually married and had two children, Bob and May.

When his two children were young, his wife died; and he moved to Chicago, where he met Grandma Dorothy at a community dance. They fell in love and married, even though Grandpa towered over her. He was taller than six feet, while she was maybe five feet—in heels! Grandma took care of her step children, Bob and May, until she had Aunt Carol. Aunt Carol was a very sick baby, and so Bob and May went to live with their family in Indiana.

Dad, James Lee Carlson, was born in 1926. Until he was five, his family lived at 101st and State Street in Roseland, an area of Chicago, in their two-flat building, a blend of a single-family house and an apartment. Grandma and Grandpa rented out one floor to another family as an investment.

When Dad was two, Aunt Carol was born. She was a colicky baby, so Dad took haven with Grandma's sister, Aunt Anne, for almost a year. Aunt Anne, who Dad remembers fondly, later married and had a son named Paul. Dad and Paul grew up together and were very close during their childhoods. They always kept in touch, even when Paul lived further away.

Jim, on the right, with his sister, Carol, in front of their home in Roseland, in Illinois, 1929.

We saw Uncle Paul several times a year when we were growing up in Chicago. We even visited Paul and his wife, Ginger, in Kalamazoo, Michigan when Larry was a teenager. He gave our family Unicap vitamins, which were tiny brown pills that looked like peas. Uncle Paul worked for Unicap, and sent me postcards from Japan, where he went on business trips. When I had an assignment in the 5th grade, to make something about a foreign country, I made a book about Japan using the postcards. Uncle Paul liked children, and could make us laugh easily.

When the Depression hit in 1929, Grandpa lost his job, and the tenant couldn't pay the rent. So, they lost the house, and moved nearby into the first floor of a two-flat white frame house. Grandpa and Grandma rented there until Grandpa died of a stroke in 1963, at 75 years old. He had a series of strokes over the years, and was forced to retire early. Even when their livelihood improved after the Depression, Grandpa was afraid to buy a house.

After Grandpa was hurt in a terrible car accident, he stopped driving because he believed it was too dangerous. Instead, they used streetcars, buses, and trains. Once Dad got his license and purchased a car, he drove the family on longer trips.

Grandma Dorothy, who was thin and wiry, loved to walk. The stores in Roseland were not far from their house. Grandma was also well read and intelligent.

When Ron met Grandma, she was in her eighties and living with my Aunt Carol, Uncle Clary, and my five cousins in South Holland, Illinois. She always impressed everyone with her knowledge of world events and her love of life. In fact, she lived to be ninety-four years old, which was fairly unusual back then. She kept up with the news from newspapers, read books often, and helped Aunt Carol and my mom with household chores.

She disclosed her secret to a long life: her grandchildren keeping her active. Grandma would stay with us in Dolton, and babysit when my parents went out. We played a game where she hid the keys in plain sight and we would have to find them, and card games of crazy eights and rummy. She always asked about the books we were reading and our school projects.

Roseland was a melting pot of nationalities, including Italian, Polish, Lithuanian, Swedish, and Canadian. Dad knew a tad of each language. In those days, community meant everybody knew and helped each other. Grandma Dorothy helped the neighbors, some of whom were Swedish and some Polish. Although many of the immigrants learned to speak English, their reading skills weren't as strong. So, Grandma would translate letters and give them advice.

The Depression thrust the country into survival mode. Not only did jobs die, but the principles upon which the country was founded were challenged. No longer were hard work, reliability, and integrity enough to secure your future. However, hope persisted, thanks to the creativity and leadership of the Franklin Delano Roosevelt administration. A work relief program focusing on environmental projects, called Civilian Conservation Corps, was part of Roosevelt's solution to the anarchy and despair that swept the nation.

Grandpa was one of the first to sign up to the corps in 1933. He helped rebuild the streetcar tracks that snaked across Chicago. Ron remembers the tracks in the sixties, although electric buses were more common then. Those buses were still hooked to the overhead electric lines, even though they used tires instead of tracks.

To contribute to the family, Dad got a job at a greenhouse and nursery when he was eleven. He dragged and shoveled dirt, planted seedlings, and built supports.

He became close friends with the owners until he joined the Navy at seventeen. He ended up tapping his nursery experience when we planted a backyard garden at our Dolton home, when I was ten. We planted leaf lettuce, carrots, peas and eventually radishes to keep the rabbits away from our other plants. He also grew rhubarb and raspberries. I liked working in the garden with Dad, and eating the sweet peas right out of the pods. My mom would send me out to pick the leaf lettuce for our salads for dinner. Every place I lived we have planted flowers, and sometimes vegetables. In Cincinnati, I asked my Dad why he didn't have a garden and he said. "because you aren't here to help me with it." That made me feel really special.

For recreation as a child, Dad loved to play baseball and marbles, and he walked a mile or more to Pullman Park during the summers to swim. He and his best friend, Claude Bergstrand, worked as lifeguards in high school, during the summers at the YMCA. They also tried to sell Liberty Magazine subscriptions door to door, but most people weren't interested. After work, they binged on as many mini square hamburgers as their money could buy at White Castle.

Claude's father retired around the time Claude entered the service for WWII, and their family moved to northern Minnesota. They lived on a lake in the woods, about fifty miles from Duluth. They built a log cabin, and a few one-room cabins to rent out during the summer. Claude moved up there after the service. He was one of the lucky ones who never saw combat, or even left the country. When I was in high school, Mom, Dad, and Jeannette and I visited the June and Claude Bergstrand in Duluth twice. We really enjoyed the cooler weather, quiet peacefulness, canoeing on the lake and visiting with Claude, his wife June, and their sons, Jon and Glenn. They came to Chicago to visit with us a few times, and we enjoyed having them. June baked bread, made pancakes, great dinners and luscious desserts. She was a very happy lady with a great sense of humor, and I think she enjoyed having girls in her house for a change. We went on picnics and watched June and Claude square dance at the Firehouse, which served as a community center.

After the Depression, Grandpa made passenger train cars for the Pullman Company. As an accomplished machinist and welder, he could make anything out of steel. Before the country set safety regulations, Grandpa, along with many others, lost much of his hearing after long-term work in a loud factory. Grandma also developed hearing trouble as she aged. Unfortunately, Grandpa's large hearing aids didn't help much. I remember sitting on his lap as he watched Chicago teams play baseball on TV. Although he couldn't hear the commentators, he loved watching as they sang "Let's Go, Go-Go White Sox"

Church was another activity of Dad's youth. He would walk a few blocks with his sister, Aunt Carol, to Emmanuel Reformed Church, but their parents seldom accompanied them. Instead, Grandpa listened to the Swedish Lutheran church service on the radio at home. Occasionally, Grandma walked eight or more blocks to the Methodist church. She was raised Presbyterian. I asked Dad why he and Aunt Carol went to Emmanuel, and he said it was close by and had a good Sunday School program that was very friendly to children.

Dad was around fifteen when America entered the war, and he joined the Reserve Officer Training Corps, known as ROTC, in high school. While not as determined to fight as some, Dad believed in the cause. Instead of waiting to be drafted, he enlisted with the Navy at seventeen to have more control. He thought fighting from a ship would be preferable to hand-to-hand combat.

After basic training, Dad's test scores indicated he was a candidate for advanced training. At Signalman school, he graduated in the top 10 percent of the class, and was sent to learn the signals of other countries to facilitate communication with their ships. Upon completing his schooling, he was put on leave for a few days before receiving his combat orders.

I am sure that Grandma and Grandpa Carlson and Aunt Carol were nervous about Dad's going overseas. They were a very close family, and I am sure certain they already knew of families that had lost family members in WWII. The war had dragged on, and everyone wanted it to end as soon as possible. I also think that Dad's ROTC training in high school, and his strong work ethic, helped him to achieve his status in the Navy; but he had never ventured outside of America. It was going to be an adventure that he would never forget.

Mary Jane Meets Jim

When she was twenty, Mom had a premonition that something special was going to happen the day she met Dad. She did something unusual that morning: She bought a pretty white stylish blouse. Money was tight, so Grandma made most of her clothes that weren't hand-me-downs from relatives.

Her cousin asked Mom to go to a USO dance in Kenosha that night, where they often went to meet servicemen. Where else could a young woman meet men during the war? In addition, Mom was writing a stream of letters to many of the servicemen she met.

For some reason, Grandma and Grandpa Johnson didn't want her to go that night. Her cousin, however, insisted. Well, Mom hadn't bought that blouse for nothing, and couldn't wait to wear it, so they went anyway.

Meanwhile, Dad, after much training, had a few days of leave. He wanted to go to the Milwaukee USO, but a fellow sailor wanted to go to Kenosha instead. Naturally, they did the mature thing: They flipped a coin. Dad lost.

Once Dad saw the young women gracing the club that night, he understood why his friend had preferred Kenosha. As he scanned the room, he spotted Mom poised on a couch. She was thin, with her dark page boy hair and pretty blue eyes. And of course, she was dressed like a doll in a skirt, and of course, her new blouse.

Years later after I was grown up and married, Dad told me he felt as if God had guided him to approach her. So, he walked suavely over to her couch, and knocked over a standing lamp, which she caught. That was how they met.

That night, they talked and talked—and talked. It was obvious to Mom that he wasn't a lady's man. As a nineteen-year-old sailor, Dad had little dating experience. His nerves wouldn't have allowed him to deliver a smooth line if he had known one! But he did what he knew how to do: He fired a barrage of questions at her.

Dad found her fascinating and wanted to know her every detail. Mom said he must have asked fifty questions. Instead of dancing, they played chess. Dad's strategy was to impress her with his mastery of the game… until she won. Somehow, though, losing to her didn't bother him.

At the end of the night, Dad asked her to write to him. She offered a twist: "Write me first and I'll answer." Too many servicemen hadn't written her back, but she sensed and hoped he would be different. He was.

After three to four hours of talking—or rather interrogation—they departed excited over their special night together. Dad may have lost the coin toss, but he apparently had won Mom's heart.

Back on his base, Great Lakes Naval Station in Illinois, that very evening, Dad's orders had arrived. He would leave on a troop train the very next morning for the West Coast.

From there, Dad was assigned to the Pacific Fleet, as the main signalman for a transport ship, that would move men and equipment.

He would not see Mom again for almost two years.

Sailor Without a Ship

Dad was not a typical swabbie. He didn't smoke or drink or chase women. He was, however, true to his word. He started writing to Mom immediately. One of his first letters began as follows:

> July 17, 1945
>
> Dear Mary Jane,
>
> Congratulations. It's our anniversary, you know. It was one week ago today that I met you. Now I am 2,400 miles away and can't see you, but I can dream and remember. It was so wonderful it almost doesn't seem real. I shall never forget it.

Frequent letters like this to each other bonded them through the next year. In fact, mom always told me that they fell in love long distance.

Dad didn't get the letters in a timely fashion, though, because the Navy often moved him. Plus, the letters were censored; the military refused to take the chance that the enemy could learn anything from intercepted mail. Dad said, he knew the serviceman in his unit who reviewed their letters; and he hated censoring his fellow soldier's mail, even though he realized it was necessary.

Dad's assignment as a signalman was not without risks. He worked on the highest bridge of the ship, as it transferred troops and supplies to the front. During attacks, the enemy aimed for his bridge. He couldn't leave the bridge without orders during any high level of alert.

It was October when Dad's ship, the USS Feland, an attack transport, arrived in the Philippines. The crew disembarked on Samar island, just above the island of Leyte, for a short R&R. He ventured off with some shipmates to explore the jungle. Distracted by the allure of beautiful, exotic flowers and plants, and unusual, persistent animal noises, the sailors became disoriented. One trail looked like another. The ship's departure time came and went without them. They started to discuss their limited survival training.

Dad always seemed anxious about getting lost. He would quiz Ron about where he was taking me, and how we were getting there. I think this stemmed from his misadventure in the jungle. Mom was just the opposite. She viewed getting lost as an adventure, where we could see more places, and possibly meet interesting people. She calmed Dad down on many of our trips.

Although the group was only lost for a few hours, it seemed much longer to Dad. They ended up running into a group of Marines in the jungle. Their relief was short lived. The commander, who was aware of the Feland's departure, reassigned them to the Marines—in hand-to-hand jungle combat. Back then, the Marines were considered a branch of the Navy. Of course, they had no need for a master signalman.

In addition to their ability to annoy, the island's mosquitoes could impart a little gift to their victims. When Dad developed a rash, fever, headache, muscle and joint pain, the corpsman gave him the good news: dengue fever. This meant a two-week stay on the nearest hospital ship before he could return to his jungle unit.

Soon after, Dad took on a commitment that he would regret. One of his acquaintances on the island asked if he would be the new master of his pet monkey, Peggy. Lured by the novelty, Dad agreed. Peggy followed him everywhere—and got into a lot of trouble.

While everyone snoozed at night in their tent, Peggy would start her shenanigans. The men woke up to messes everywhere. Curiosity was one of Peggy's predominant traits. Neat footlockers had been ravaged, and clothing set out for the morning was found outside. Plus, it's hard to potty-train a monkey! It wasn't long before Dad started to question his decision, but Peggy was very affectionate to him. He and his bunk mates had kept Peggy a secret. She was cute and entertaining.

The servicemen, including Dad's friends, received coupons for beer, and some of the guys sneaked beer to Peggy without telling Dad. Who knew, apparently monkeys love beer! Soon everyone fell asleep, except you know who. In the middle of the night, the staggering monkey grabbed a loaded pistol and fired it. Fortunately, no one got hurt, but the MPs (military police) showed up with guns drawn. When they discovered it was a monkey, Peggy was dishonorably discharged. Dad gave her to a local Philippine man, who took Peggy back into the jungle, far away from camp.

During the time that Dad kept Peggy, he wrote to Mom about her, and even signed Peggy's paw prints on his letters. Of course, Mom and her family found the monkey stories hysterical! I think we need humor the most when things are serious. Dad's sense of humor has been one of his trademarks.

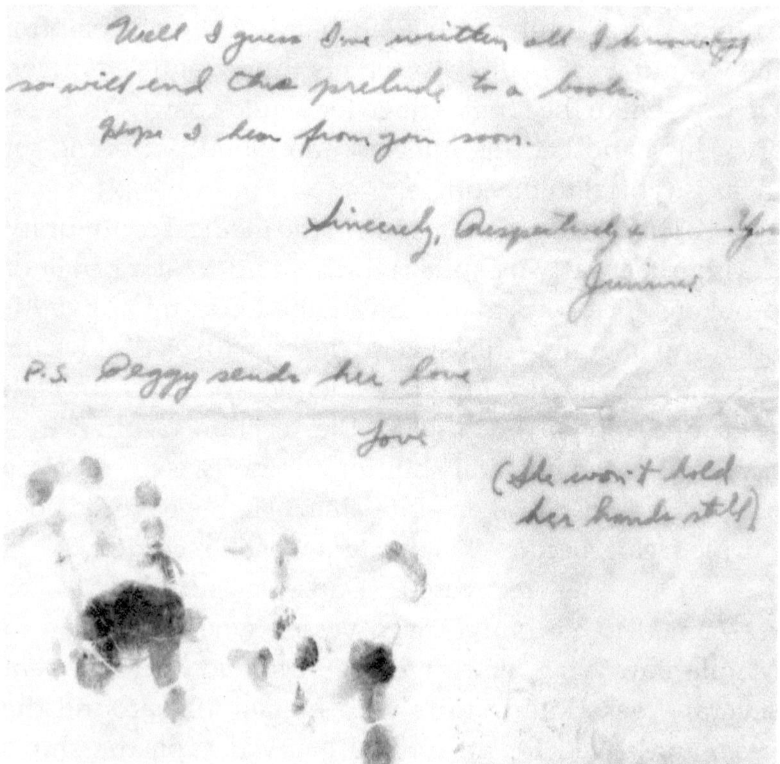

Well I guess I've written all I know
so will end this prelude to a book.
Hope I hear from you soon.

Sincerely, Respectfully & —— Yours
Jimmie

P.S. Peggy sends her love
Love
(She won't hold
her hands still)

Jim Carlson sent this letter with his monkey's paw prints to his future wife, Mary Jane, from the Philippines during World War II.

Dad's reputation as a fighter, though, was less sterling. If it doesn't sound like a great idea to randomly assign a sailor to jungle fighting, it wasn't. Dad knew how to use his rifle, pistol, and rather large knife... in theory. Swabbies, especially in the signal corps, weren't highly trained in hand-to-hand combat. Dad admitted to us that, while he was skilled at a deck-mounted 20 mm gun on a ship, he "couldn't hit the broad side of a barn" with handheld weapons. He also was somewhat low on the gung-ho factor, which seems prevalent in Marine lore.

During one of his early encounters with dissident forces, Dad did well, meaning he survived. However, he caught a stray bullet in his left hand. Although painful, the wound was small, between his thumb and forefinger. He was sent to the jungle triage for a quick patch job. Soon after, his hand became infected and blood poisoning set in, as is typical in the jungle.

The latest, greatest thing in the medical community during that war was sulfa, which could treat a range of problems. The corpsman who stitched Dad up applied it often and liberally. After several doses, with Dad's luck (or lack thereof), he developed an allergic reaction. Although sulfa probably saved his life, the reaction resulted in a trip back to the hospital ship for another week. Needless to say, Dad hasn't taken sulfa since. He never received a Purple Heart, because his incident wasn't recorded.

Once he recovered, Dad was thrilled to be reassigned to YF-246, a cargo vessel, when it docked in Manila Bay. When he arrived, YF-246 had not. He spent several weeks killing time with menial jobs around the base, and asked for an update every day on the ship's location.

Just when he was starting to question the ship's very existence, he received one final report: The vessel had been destroyed, along with much of its crew. I reflect on this sometimes when I'm late for something, or get lost. We never know when we are being protected. God obviously had better things in store for Dad than for those unfortunate YF-246 shipmates.

Dad next reported to the company commander in Manila. He thought Dad might have a better calling than jungle warfare, and offered him a position in shop management. Dad can organize anything. As a kid, he probably categorized and numbered his marbles.

Dad thrived in his new duties. He was thankful he had a good job, was reasonably safe, and was gaining vocational training for his eventual career in accounting.

In Manila, Dad bumped into Herman Draught, one of his sister Carol's boyfriends from Roseland. He was a Navy butcher on the island, and interacted with Dad professionally and personally. I don't think Dad disclosed everything to Mom. One time when Dad and Herman were at the base's USO, Dad met a local woman named Gloria. Her father was the former mayor of Manila, and Dad enjoyed spending time with Gloria and her family. Their relationship was casual, though.

Jim Carlson, left, and Herman Draught were friends in Manila, the Philippines, in 1945 during World War II.

Near the war's end, Dad received orders to ship to Luzon, at the northern end of the Philippines, with the Marines to invade Japan. This scheduled assault was to be akin to D-Day in Europe, a final drive across the mainland of Japan to force a Japanese surrender.

Jim Carlson was a signalman in
Manila in the Philippines during WWII.

Jim Carlson on bow of a ship In Manila during WWII.

Fortunately, this was just a plan B. Japan ignored warnings, and nuclear weapons, developed during the Manhattan Project, were dropped on Hiroshima on August 6 and Nagasaki on August 9, 1945. Japan surrendered, and ended the war in the Pacific. We have cringed at the pictures of the devastation. While we don't know, and refuse to debate the cost in lives compared to continued conflict, in our family, we are grateful Dad remained safe.

Finally, Dad could relax, but the military didn't release him from duty. He almost enjoyed the routine duties on the ship ride back to the States. Obviously, Dad was excited about returning home, and seeing his family and Mom. However, the Navy had different plans.

When his cruiser arrived in San Francisco, Dad was whisked to the Navy base on Yerba Buena Island in San Francisco Bay. He became a master-at-arms at the barracks, which is a petty officer, similar to civilian police. On shore patrol, he mostly protected sailors from civilians who would swindle them out of their money.

On the side, he learned leatherwork from a woman who taught servicemen at the USO. She gave him a set of tools when he departed, and Dad continued to enjoy leatherwork over the years, especially in Cincinnati after he retired. We appreciate the purses, belts, wallets, and other beautiful items he has crafted for us.

After several months in that assignment, Dad was transferred to the Navy prison in Northern California to deal with serious offenders. He carried a baton, a .45 pistol and handcuffs. Dad didn't savor serving as a prison guard, or Navy policeman, but the armed forces didn't give him a choice.

While in California, Dad continued his frequent correspondence with Mom, but they weren't reunited until Dad finally was released from active duty in July of 1946.

Jim Carlson was a master-at-arms in San Francisco after WWII.

Reunited

After two years away, Dad returned home to Chicago in late summer of 1946, for inactive duty. He continued his education at the University of Illinois's Navy Pier campus. During the war the 3300-foot structure, which jutted out into Lake Michigan, was used as a Navy training facility. He attended the college's very first class on the GI Bill, while working a part-time job. He decided to major in chemical engineering, because he thought it would be profitable, and he had excelled in high-school chemistry.

We know what you're thinking—the same thing Dad was. What about Mom? One of the first things he did was call her to plan a date. They loved each other, but didn't know each other intimately. Somehow letters and phone calls eventually fall a little short.

Dad would board trains, buses, dogsleds—whatever it took to reach Wisconsin. Okay, he didn't use dogsleds, but he took a bus to downtown Chicago and a train to Kenosha. Then he walked the last half mile from the train station. The whole process usually took two to three hours.

Their first date was on a Saturday. He left at the crack of dawn and returned in the evening. Dad didn't mind the long day, though, and Mom was thrilled. Dad was finally real, and turned out to be the same endearing person who had filled her imagination since their three-hour meeting. Her parents could sense immediately, that Dad was a good man, and would be the right fit for Mom. They also felt they knew him from his letters.

Ron often wondered how much you can truly learn about someone through the mail. We have seen the boxes of letters—yes, plural—in their basement. It's a wonder that they had time to do anything else!

After their first date, Mom and Dad's courtship finally began in earnest. Initially, Dad did the traveling. The fifty or so miles would not be an obstacle, nor would Mom's full-time secretarial job, or Dad's classes. They saw each other at least every other week. Their dates became the priority, and most anticipated parts of their lives.

They enjoyed walks, strolls to the park, dancing to the music of the big bands, movies, and visiting friends. Their Cinderella hour was 9:00 p.m., when Grandpa Johnson would wind the clock in front of them and say, "It's getting late." Dad must have hated that. Ron can empathize, because Dad used a similar tactic when he started dating me. Ah, tradition.

Once Grandma and Grandpa grew to trust Dad, they let him spend the night. This allowed more time with Mom. He slept with Mom's younger brother, Uncle Cliff, who was about eight years old.

Dad has always been extremely family oriented. He and Mom often included her parents in their plans. Apparently, a visit by a boyfriend was a big occasion in Kenosha! Like Ron, Dad was a little overwhelmed by the siblings, aunts, uncles, cousins, and grandparents, etc. Occasionally, even Mom would get frustrated at her family for intruding on her time with Dad.

Eventually, Dad's mother, Grandma Dorothy, mailed a letter to Grandma and Grandpa Johnson to invite

Mom to Chicago. Just like Mom's parents, Grandma and Grandpa Carlson recognized their compatibility. After that, they took turns visiting each other, but Dad still shouldered the majority of the traveling.

In Kenosha, Mom and Dad hopped the streetcars to go out, or occasionally caught a ride with a friend or neighbor. On the streetcar, Mom would talk to the driver like she had known him for years. Afterward, Dad would say, "Why didn't you introduce me to your friend?" Then Mom would reveal that she didn't know him, which upset Dad. With her open, trusting nature, Mom would talk to anyone.

They talked about marriage soon after Dad returned from the war, realizing they wanted to be together forever.

In the summer, Dad would accompany Mom, Grandma and Grandpa Johnson, and her siblings to Silver Lake on weekend trips, not far from Kenosha. They used a cabin that belonged to my Great Uncle Ed. The men fished while the women visited and cooked. They would eat what they caught at every meal.

We think Dad slept on the floor with the other men. It wasn't really a vacation for him; he and Mom were never alone. Eventually, Dad tired of all things fish. We are quite sure Mom was the only reason he endured those trips. After that, the only time Dad went fishing again was with his friend, Claude, in Minnesota.

For the most part, Mom and Dad were very happy together. They danced to the big bands that toured through Chicago and Kenosha. Mom's friends clicked with Dad immediately. But of course, no one loved Dad as much as Mom. When I asked Mom how she knew that Dad was "The One", Mom said she wasn't able to visualize her life without him. She believed God had brought them together.

Dad had survived the war, dengue fever, hand-to-hand combat, a gunshot, infection, and had dodged dying on a destroyed ship. It was time for happily ever after, right? What could go wrong?

Winter in Chicago can be a hazardous time. One blustery December day, the snow was falling so rapidly that Dad could barely see across the street. He was dashing off the IC (Illinois Central Railroad) to catch a waiting bus, and failed to see the car racing along the snow-crusted street. The driver didn't spot Dad until it was too late.

The car hit him, and Dad flew through the windshield. He was rushed to Edward Jr. Hines VA Hospital, where he was not fully conscious for several days. When Mom arrived, the doctors said he faced a 50/50 chance of survival.

After several days in intensive care, when internal bleeding had lessened, the concern shifted to his mental state. His face had endured quite a blow, and the doctors weren't certain how much brain damage he might have suffered. Dad had retrograde amnesia, and couldn't remember a lot of the past. Fortunately, he did remember Mom and his parents. However, he thought he was still in the Navy, and repeatedly asked about the war.

Mom's family was distraught, they couldn't get married because of the accident. Some people believed they would never marry, but their love was strong. From the moment they had met, they believed they were meant to be together. Obviously, this was hard on Mom. The trip by train and streetcars wasn't the simplest commute, but Mom was determined to stay by Dad's side.

Mary Jane Johnson after WWII.

Jim and Mary Jane, ready for a date after WWII.

Even though Dad was still in the hospital, Mom lugged a heavy waffle iron through the icy streets of Chicago as a Christmas gift. That was on her list of dumbest decisions ever. Mom kept thinking, she could die if she slipped and it landed on her. I'm sure Dad probably would have been happier if she had just brought some waffles. He savored her cooking.

Dad finally was released after six weeks, but he had to return multiple times during the next year for procedures. Thankfully, he doesn't remember everything he had to endure, but facial reconstruction took quite a bit of time. None of this changed the way Mom felt about Dad. If he never looked like the handsome young sailor she had met, he was still her man.

What did bother them, though, was his suffering from double vision and migraines. The doctors had done as much as possible with their surgical technology at the time, but they couldn't align his eyes properly, or completely repair the nerve damage.

As a little girl, I heated up washrags to apply to his eyes when he returned home from work. Dealing with numbers, and reading in his job in billing caused strain on his eyes and headaches. I hated seeing him in such pain. Thankfully, a final surgery corrected the problem, when I was in high school.

Their official engagement that first year after the accident was almost anticlimactic. When Dad asked Mom, she emphatically said yes. No ring or kneeling. We've never heard of a couple with less doubt than Mom and Dad.

Similar to Ron's parents, their engagement involved no pomp and circumstance. Considering how successful their marriages were, maybe that's the way it should be. Think about that before you propose on the big screen at the ballpark. When two people are truly compatible, they don't need all the dramatic frills.

Once he recovered most of his memory from one to two years after the accident, Dad resumed his focus on college and future plans. He decided to take some recently developed aptitude and interest tests at University of Chicago, to ensure he was in the right field, the results indicated he would make a mediocre chemical engineer, but a great accountant. So, Dad changed his major, and took accounting and business classes at the Navy Pier. He worked at the post office at night, and took public transportation to get home.

In May 1950, Mom and Dad were married at Mom's Congregational Church in Kenosha. Their friend, the milkman (yes, they still existed), sang during the morning ceremony. Claude had scheduled his own wedding the week before, so he could serve as Dad's best man, but it snowed too much for Claude to trek from northern Minnesota. So, Mom's sister, Joann's fiancé, Uncle Dale, stepped up as best man.

Mom borrowed a lovely white A-line dress from her cousin, and her four bridesmaids, including Aunt Helen, wore pastel colors. Aunt Joann was the maid of honor.

A small reception in the fellowship hall, with cake and punch followed the ceremony. Afterward, Grandma Johnson hosted a luncheon for the bridal party, and relatives at her home. As usual, she cooked most of the dishes.

Mom and Dad traveled to the Ozark Mountains in Arkansas for their honeymoon. It was sweltering, but they still enjoyed it. They said the people talked and moved slow, but were hospitable and friendly.

When they returned to Chicago, they lived with Grandma and Grandpa Carlson, in their two-flat rental in

Roseland, but eventually got an apartment. Mom worked in an office during the day, while Dad toiled at the post office at night. The job gave him an ulcer.

At first, Mom cooked enough delicious food for seven people, because she was accustomed to cooking for her large family; but both of them were rail thin. A hectic schedule of college and work burned their calories.

Their favorite dates involved big bands and dancing, particularly at the Trianon Ballroom on Cottage Grove Avenue, in Chicago. It drew some of the best talent in the area for Lawrence Welk-style shows. Getting there was not easy, though. The streetcar and bus schedules didn't synchronize well. Often, they had to wait for the bus, in a graveyard, in the middle of the night, as Dad put it.

Their dance nights were interrupted when Mom fell over a curb and broke a foot. She propped her foot on a box at the office and kept working. Six months later, she broke her other foot when a bicyclist hit her. Unfortunately, Mom coped with foot problems the rest of her life, which limited her walking (When Ron met her, he noticed her swollen feet). She ended up resigning from her job, not only because of her feet, but also to spend time with Dad, because their work schedules didn't align. Dad bought her a TV to help fill her time. Mom always love watching TV especially soap operas, game shows like the Match Game, and comedies like I Love Lucy, That Girl and the Donna Reed Show. She also watched Dinah Shore and Merv Griffin's variety shows, which would have singing, dancing, and interviews with stars.

Dad ended up quitting college after mom stopped working, to allow for a full-time job. Mom felt guilty about his sacrifice, but knew he was determined to take care of her.

Dad had worked in the mailroom of Sherwin-Williams, the paint company, when he was younger, and knew the manager. He sometime later landed a good job, in the billing department, and learned more about accounting. Eventually, Dad helped install and updated their computer systems. He retired after three decades.

Their parenting phase began in November 1953, when my brother Larry was born. I arrived nineteen months later in June 1955, followed by Jeannette four years later, in June 1959. Mom and Dad were great parents. Dad was the typical strict, but caring father, while Mom defined caring and nurturing. I know Mom and Dad were meant to be together and to be parents.

Left to right, Larry, Jeannette, Jim, Mary Jane, and Crystal in the Carlsons' Christmas card, circa 1963.

IV

About Marriage

Ron

When we began putting words to paper fifteen years ago, this work was intended to honor our parents' memories by sharing their stories with our children and grandchildren. We came to realize that the world needs the examples and message of this book.

Our journey, through 150 years of history, covering the world, from the Philippines to Europe and America in not only interesting but demonstrates the value of commitment to marriage and resulting family happiness. We hope that these three real-life stories will serve as examples and inspiration that "till death" commitments and lasting love stories can be more than dreams.

To complete our mission and encourage those who have shared our stories and message, we offer our insights into marriage. From the beginning, God intended this institution to be for our own good. Where have we gone wrong? Why, in so many ways, does it seem to fail these days? What do we need to do for marriage to succeed?

While marriage isn't for everyone, with commitment and some effort, it can bring great peace and joy for 'as long as you both shall live.'

ENDING WELL

Crystal

Mom and Mimi had one thing in common: Neither wanted to outlive their spouse. In an odd sense, that means they won.

Mom died at eighty years old in March 2006 – eleven years before Dad. Actually, if someone had told us she would live that long, we would have been skeptical, because of her health issues. She had survived multiple illnesses. She had a neurological disease, which defied proper diagnosis. She suffered migraines, and occasionally a severe equilibrium problem. She had poor circulation in her legs and brittle bones. Over the years she broke her back, hip, leg, and both feet.

Despite her suffering, she was the most positive, happiest person you could ever meet. Of course, sometimes she felt depressed; but often she called people or wrote letters, which seemed to eliminate those feelings. She shared her unshakable faith in God with us, her friends, and acquaintances. Her laughter punctuated funny stories as she entertained people.

For the last few years of her life, my dad was Mom's caretaker. Confined to a wheelchair, she needed help doing almost everything. However, it didn't break her spirit or faith, always ready with sage advice for Ron and me. We would talk on the phone for hours.

Dad never complained, but the experience was obviously overwhelming. He was a true example of love in action. Confinement and codependence made them a bit snippier, though. Mom, much as Mimi, lamented dependence and loss of her role. Dad struggled to do the things she physically needed, and probably isolated her more than she wanted. He was always afraid he wouldn't be able to move her in and out of the car, or that she would fall.

Ron and I visited as often as possible (about every six to eight weeks). Ron was a great help to Dad and Mom. He could manage getting her into and out of the wheelchair, so we took her out to dinner or to quilt shops or bookstores. Larry and his wife, Linda, lived much closer and helped them with everything.

On March 9, 2006, Linda called to tell us Mom was close to death from a final bout of pneumonia. As I was showering to get ready to leave, I heard Mom call my name. Ron probably drove the two hundred miles to Cincinnati a little faster than normal in our relative silence. Would we get there in time? Regardless, we had to help Dad.

I will never forget that dark evening when we arrived. Dad was leaving the nursing home, after spending most of the day there. Mom was unconscious, and he knew she wouldn't last long. We are certain, as we had witnessed before, he told her the news of the day, as if she would wake up to respond.

Minutes later, we walked into her hospice room to see flowers and plants everywhere. Under different circumstances, the room would have inspired compliments for its peaceful, and tasteful décor. However, the bed drew our eyes to where Linda sat crying, and Larry was behind comforting her.

"She's gone," Linda said, looking up.

Mom had waited for Dad to finish his visit. Somehow, even though unconscious in our world, she had told God to wait just a few minutes longer.

Linda rose to greet us, and we all talked for a few minutes. Ron sat next to Mom, and held her wrist checking her pulse. Although she had stopped breathing, her heart continued to beat for about another minute. He took that opportunity to thank God for her life, and for ending her suffering. He also prayed for Dad, and felt confident his prayer would be answered.

We drove to their house to tell dad in person. Dad and I held each other and cried. We were going to miss her so much!

Later, Dad said he couldn't have survived the funeral, and the following days and months, without the love of his children and their spouses. We continued to visit whenever possible. He never got over her loss, but kept living his life the best he could.

He had friends who checked on him, neighbors who took care of some of his needs, and a nursing and cleaning service. Larry and Linda talked to him frequently, took him to church, ate with him often, and helped with doctor appointments and anything he needed.

It may be the result of a marriage that lasted for fifty-five years, but Dad insisted he still felt Mom's presence in the house. With confidence and eagerness, he looked forward to the day they would be reunited. He spoke as though it was an undeniable certainty. How comforting it must be to hold that level of faith.

In his last year of life, Dad lived in a nursing home near Larry's house. He had lost a great deal of weight, and then broke his leg. He always welcomed us when we visited. It made me feel good to hold his hand and say, "I love you, Daddy." In return, he would say, "I love you" and thanked us for coming.

Dad went home to be with Jesus on Feb. 16, 2017, after a stroke. The next morning, our granddaughter, Addy, was born. It felt like the Bible verse, "Sorrow lasts for a night, but joy comes in the morning." (Psalm 30:5). Elizabeth brought Addy a week later to the funeral, and our relatives passed her around in admiration. Dad loved babies, and I think he appreciated that.

As the graveside ceremony with full military honors began, it started to snow. The Navy personnel were underdressed for it, like most of us. They never showed it, though. The wind picked up as the trumpet played taps, and Ron had to help hold the flag on the casket.

Dad had finally gotten his wish. He was once again, and forever more will be, with the love of his life.

Every so often, we smell his pipe smoke in our house, so we know he is checking up on us. We are grateful he and Mom got the opportunity to read the early draft of our memoir, and were excited about it.

Letting Go

Ron

My Mom died in January of 2012 at the age of 87. In the hospital, I told dad when it was time to let her go. They stopped treatment, and she slipped away later that evening. Mom, as she had my whole life, made even that decision easier. After months of slow decline; she told me 'please just let me die. Everyone has to die you know.' Crystal and I were at her bedside early the next morning. I stroked her hair, and dabbed her with a little Chanel #5 (her perfume of choice) I found in a drawer. Dad was definitely sad and disillusioned. Somehow, he always thought mom would eventually be cured and return home.

Crystal and I stayed to help with the funeral. I helped him make decisions about the funeral and service. Dad was in no condition to make those on his own. The services were held in their home town of Oak Lawn, Illinois. Dad was amazed at the turnout. For a couple who stayed mainly to themselves, they had a lot of friends and neighbors. Of the two, mom was definitely the more social. I also saw friends of my childhood, with whom I haven't even kept in contact. Everyone could recall mom's hospitality: dinners, snacks, the cookies and Kool Aide after play, and the friendly greetings. None of her eccentricities, or awkward encounters seemed to be remembered. Our daughters and granddaughter cried. Dad was cordial, but somewhat stoic.

While life went on and we soon moved him closer to us in Columbus, Ohio, he was never the same after Mimi died. We had many good times, over the next seven years, after he moved to Ohio, but something in him was missing. I think that is one of the curses of a long marriage. I remember in our marriage ceremony, the pastor said 'and the two shall become one.' I could see with both of our fathers that, when they lost their wives somehow, they seemed less than whole.

Dad died in May 2019 at the age of ninety-eight. Our pastor, Rod Uhlig (pastor of the Burt Avenue Wesleyan Church in Coshocton, Ohio), asked if I wanted to say anything at the memorial service. I felt as if I had to, and am glad I wrote it down. I have always been a better writer than public speaker. While I managed not to cry, I had to stop several times to keep my emotions in check. This was what I read.

> I never knew Dad when he was in the Army during World War II, or when he stood up in his jeep to yell at a young German woman who had lost track of time, and was out after the military curfew. I was there, however, to hear her yell back on numerous occasions, during their sixty-four years of marriage.
>
> Mom and Dad had, let's call it, an exciting relationship. But beneath the occasional friction, they had a bond of love never to be broken. Dad never missed a day visiting her at the rehab center those last 6 months. When she passed in January 2012, he felt totally lost. At ninety-one, he owned a nice three-bedroom house—the house I grew up in—with a yard

that was the envy of the neighborhood. But it became increasingly difficult for him to take care of it. He had friends in the neighborhood, but no best friends and no family.

That fall, we sold his house and moved him to his new apartment in New Albany, Ohio. While life would never again be the same, he at least could construct a new life and be near family. Every day, weather permitting, he would walk two miles through the beautiful nearby metro park, Blendon Woods. He did his own shopping, cooking, laundry, etc. He at least had a life again.

Dad was a proud man, and self-sufficiency was important. I believe the expression, "Pride cometh before the fall," was written with him in mind. That included the fall he took at ninety-three years old in 2014, when he broke his hip getting out of the swimming pool. He refused to use his cane, as we had warned him numerous times.

Throughout his rehab and subsequent move to assisted living, we continued to offer him all of the support we could. We visited multiple times each week and took him for walks, rides, and meals. We included him in our family events. But, as is inevitable, he continued to decline.

If nothing else, I could tell I had made an impact in his life. I was his guy. Even in those last days of his delirium, he would stare at the ceiling while shaking and say, "Ron, you are going too fast." Another time he reached out and said, "Here, Ron, take my coat."

> But his suffering is over now, and my greatest feeling is relief. A nightmare has ended. Oh, don't get me wrong, it was a privilege to help him. I learned much more about my dad, and therein myself, in those last years than I ever thought possible. But the stress of watching a man I respected decline was undeniable. It was only through the continued support and encouragement of Crystal and my family that I could continue.

He is finally at peace and glad to be back with Mom. Somehow, Papa without Mimi never seemed quite right.

The Circle of Life

Ron

Now that our parents are gone, it is up to us to carry on the circle of life. In fact, the same month Dad died, our seventh granddaughter, Ripley Hammock, was born.

Life for Crystal and I has been an amazing adventure. Unlike our fathers, I haven't been able to keep one job for thirty years. In fact, I have held multiple jobs/careers, including chemist, lab manager, chemical plant safety coordinator, industrial supervisor, taught at the college level and substituted in elementary and high schools, and went back to school at fifty to become a registered nurse. Crystal and I also owned and operated a summer sandwich restaurant, for a couple of years. Excuse the cliché, but somehow, through it all, I have always managed to put bread on the table for Crystal, and our three wonderful daughters Elizabeth, Michelle, and Lisa. That included breadsticks crafted from outdated pizza dough, from a delivery job.

In the process, God has moved us from our original homes near Chicago, Illinois to ones in Michigan, Indiana, and finally Ohio. We joke that, we're seeing the Midwest one state at a time.

I lost jobs three times due to layoffs, because companies consolidated during economic downturns.

While working other jobs, I went back to school twice for additional degrees. I'm one of the few people who taught at an institution before receiving a degree there. I taught math before I got my nursing degree at Central Ohio Technical College.

At twenty-eight years old, I developed bladder cancer from my chemistry lab, forcing my first job/career change. It also led to our move to Michigan. It was only there, that we were led to the doctor with an experimental procedure, which cured my cancer. It still hasn't returned nearly 40 years later, thankfully. I knew God moved us for more than just a job.

At sixty-five, Crystal is also a 24+ year breast cancer survivor. She is another success story in the battle which, is all too common these days. I still remember sitting in the waiting room, with her parents during one surgery. Her dad made me nervous. He asked me questions I couldn't answer, fidgeted, and made me get periodic updates, during the nine-hour procedure. Mary Jane tried to be the calm one. I never doubted their love for their daughter. Crystal got through that surgery fine. At my side for over 42 years now, she has been the most amazing wife and mother. She has written stories, poetry, and essays. Several were published. She has also taught crafts and women's history at community college, churches and libraries. Mainly, though, she has been our family's lighthouse. Our girls still call her frequently for advice and encouragement. She has the rare gift of seeing the positives in life.

Having girls added a new level of meaning to our lives. As a young man, the thought of raising girls always scared me. Fortunately, it wound up being a pass/fail, learn as you go class, and Crystal helped greatly. I remember the pride I felt as I walked out of the hospital, carrying Elizabeth like a football. She seemed to look up and know she was safe. I never (or almost never) dropped a football. As they grew, we taught them all we could, and tried to set a good example. Today we are very proud of each of them, and the women they have become.

Our future plans include travel, helping our children and grandchildren, and continuing to write and lecture.

After forty-two anniversaries, I can say without hesitation that, marriage can work, if done right. We are the old married couple who still snuggles in the movie theater, and holds hands on the way out. We make a date out of feeding the ducks and getting ice cream. We take an overnight getaway at least three or four times a year.

Kids, don't read the following sentence: If we aren't intimate for a while, she misses it almost as much as I do. After all we have been through—and maybe because of it—we are still happy together.

As we have watched and learned from our parents, and now as our children have watched us, it is time for some perspective. Life swings as a pendulum. Slowly, one generation gives way to the next. Our lives are a constant journey from dependence to independence, and then back. All that we are passes like a wisp of vapor. However, the miracle of life continues, and with luck and effort, our lessons can be passed on. As we grow up, we never truly understand—or in some cases care—what our parents went through. I think humans are a little selfish by nature. It often isn't until we gain some life experience, that the empathy gene kicks in. I realize our families' stories don't stand out in world history, but it has been an honor to gather and share them.

I encourage you to take some time to truly delve into the lives of the people who are important to you. As I mentioned earlier, I don't always understand how God works, but it is amazing to watch.

Reflections

Ron

Although our story is done, I have had time to reflect on marriage in general. With around 50% of marriages ending in divorce, or legal separation, I'm sure many people want an answer to one question. What are the secrets to a good and long marriage? While I will be the first to admit that I'm no expert, and luck is involved, I've noticed a few clues which might be worth considering.

First and foremost, I believe it takes two complete people to have the best chance of success. Before you begin looking for 'the one', you need to focus on becoming 'the one.' In other words, don't just enjoy your single years, but take advantage of your time to become a responsible independent person. Work toward goals, independent of marital desires, that focus on optimizing your physical, mental, and spiritual health. Determine what you truly believe, what are you willing to compromise, and what is non-negotiable? Doing these things in the context of marriage will be more difficult.

Before I met Crystal, she had a specific goal of becoming a writer in Oregon. I have every confidence that if I hadn't gotten in her way, she would have followed her plan. When I met her, she was independent, and could take care of herself—an attribute I was seeking in a wife. You should too—not only in a spouse, but also yourself. I told my girls they should live on their own before marriage, and to pick a man who had done the same. Unless both of you can take care of yourselves, your relationship could become codependent and dysfunctional.

Second, pray for your future spouse, even if you don't believe in God. What are you praying for? Your answer to that question will help you determine what you want, and need in a spouse. Crystal and I did this, as you know. Make a list if that helps, like Crystal did. It is important to have a firm grasp on your expectations before emotions muddy your vision. Don't compromise your basic beliefs for anyone. If you have to, that person is not the right one.

Third, realize men and women are different. I believe the differences are part of God's plan, even if I don't understand the reasoning. Generally, men can compartmentalize their feelings, while women tend to be more empathetic, and view everything as interconnected. These complementary characteristics can make couples stronger.

Typically, a man enters marriage hoping the woman will never change. In contrast, a woman often thinks she can change her husband. However, both points of view are unrealistic. Maybe the saddest part is realizing your secret dreams will never come true. For guys, that dream might be having sex whenever and wherever they want, for the rest of their lives. For women, it may be their husbands listening to their every word, and validating everything they feel. The truth is the average guy listens for about thirty seconds before going to their happy place.

Next, try not to focus on your spouse's flaws. Instead, strive for a lifelong pursuit of becoming a better partner. With a little luck, your partner might do the same. If the trust is there, they may even ask for your help in changing some of their habits.

Make time to communicate one on one. For example, Crystal and I would take a break at a park or coffee shop almost daily, when I was working sixty to seventy hours a week. It was our time to get back in touch with each other. We also have never been shy about going to counseling. Early in our relationship, it took a third party to explain that, I needed to make our marriage the priority when it came to family obligations. Also, some of the best advice we have gotten is this cliché: Sometimes you have to agree to disagree. The priority is to be on the same team, and not to always being right. The goal should always be to win at marriage, and not at arguing.

Perhaps the most important factor in determining the length of your marriage is, choosing your partner wisely. Be analytical and not emotional. Crystal was a great example. She actually took a book out of the library, and analyzed my handwriting. My writing, while sloppy, showed no signs of deceit.

Another, and maybe better indicator of character is studying a person's relationships. For example, how does a man treat the women close to him? Does he show respect for his mother or sister? If he swears at his sister or is disrespectful to his mom, it will only be a matter of time before he treats his spouse the same way. Women can ask their social network about him. How do co-workers, friends, and even ex-girlfriends perceive him? Again, Crystal was thorough here. She first asked some of the other sisters in our fraternity. The response was unanimously good. She also talked to some of my ex-girlfriends and got no red flags.

I admit to not being nearly as thorough in my Crystal research. However, I think I got all I needed from our dating. Her idea of a great date was a walk in the park, followed by a cookie or ice cream. She also liked our Sunday date of church, followed by their pot luck dinner (students welcomed). It was obvious that Crystal was not spoiled, and had a solid set of values.

Next, infidelity is one of the main reasons marriages fail. I'm completely confident that, Crystal has been loyal to me without even asking her. I know her character, and she has spent a lot of time confronting ghosts of her past. A trusted friend of the family abused her in her youth. In light of that, I feel honored she has placed so much trust in me.

As for me, I can't deny I've been tempted on occasion. However, I instantly thought of Crystal before letting the temptation go too far.

Like any couple, we've faced rough times and disagreements, but Crystal is the only person (my mother not withstanding) who thinks more of me than I do of myself. It's not a question of losing her. I am fairly sure she would forgive me if I did stray—probably sooner than she should, in fact. We are best friends. When other women bash their husbands, she walks away and complains about it to me. She frequently brags about me to others. Even when I screw something up, she tries to rationalize why it isn't my fault. That kind of loyalty is hard to find, and should never be taken for granted, or jeopardized. We have been through so much together, but we always support and protect each other. Loyalty is a choice we make for ourselves, not for our spouse.

Finally, it's all about love. Love is the reason marriages last. This may not sound like a revelation, but let me explain.

Today, love is a misunderstood concept. We've evolved to a culture of instant gratification. Everything is geared toward maximizing our pleasure in a split second. Trust me, that is not the type of love that will make your marriage last.

Our parents got it. Sure, Jim became overwhelmed when he saw a beautiful woman, and knocked over a lamp on his way over. I assure you my dad saw more than a curfew-breaking girl when he first encountered Mimi. And I have declared my attraction to Crystal in her short poodle skirt at the college party. That's where it starts.

In the movies, boy meets girl, and all sorts of things happen—overcoming challenges, realizing they are the perfect couple, falling in love, getting married, and often that's the end of story. As small children, we are conditioned for a love story and want a fairy tale ending. There is a lot more to life than 'happily ever after.'

Be aware of the different kinds of love. The electric feeling that zaps two people together is exhilarating, but fleeting. Rather than mere infatuation, real love is not rooted in feelings, but in action. It's not about what you're looking forward to getting; it's what you're willing to give the rest of your life. If you truly believe that, and live accordingly, you'll have a 50 percent chance of a successful marriage. You can't do this by yourself, or expect a selfish partner to change. It takes two. So again, be sure about the character of your chosen partner.

I've joked to my daughters that; marriage is a life sentence. Or another cliché: Marriage is a marathon, not a sprint. This concept is foreign to today's please-me-now culture.

I'll be honest, you'll face days when you're disillusioned with your spouse, and don't feel good about your marriage. It takes an infinite amount of communication, compromise, and yes, hard work to be successful. Again, it's a choice. It's a choice we make every day, in every situation.

One problem with marriage today is that, some of these skills are best learned by example. With so many unsuccessful marriages today, children aren't seeing examples of success in their own homes.

Our parents were born between 1920 and 1926, when the United States was the dominant world power. The Great Depression hit while they were young, and an age of conservatism began. Our parents learned many ideals during this period. As they watched their own parents struggle to make ends meet, they learned to never financially overextend themselves. They never questioned the wisdom of respecting their elders. They knew hard work and integrity would lead to success. And finally, marriage was considered the ultimate partnership, and a lifelong commitment. These ideals seem outdated now, but they served my parents—and us—well throughout our lives.

Although Crystal and I grew up in different households, we share a lot of similarities. I think we learned more by our parents' examples than by the outside world. Of course, our parents fought, but divorce wasn't an option and they rarely, if ever, used it as a threat.

However, Crystal and I never doubted our parents loved each other. It was obvious in their daily actions. No matter the challenges, our parents would give each other a look of approval, a touch, or affectionate affirmation of their appreciation and love.

While times and roles are different today, mutual respect, and acts of love still work in marriage. Try it today! I believe the greatest problem in America is the need for better family values and stronger marriages. Love and stability in a marriage can help you endure whatever hardship you may face.

We hope we've provided some principles to strive toward and pass on. In conclusion, fifty-five plus sixty-four plus forty-two equals one hundred and sixty-one. We weren't quite at one hundred and fifty years when we started to write, but proceeded on faith. Faith and love are the greatest legacies we can pass down to our children.

Thank you for reading our stories. Go with God.

Jim and Mary Jane Carlson, Crystal and Ron Meinstein, Maria (Mimi) and Siegfried Meinstein. Three couples and two families officially united on our wedding day, April 1, 1978.

ACKNOWLEDGEMENTS

This memoir would not have been written without the help and encouragement of our parents, and our wonderful daughters, Elizabeth, Michelle, and Lisa. We also appreciate the support from the Coshocton Write on Writers organization, who heard Crystal read parts of this book at their meetings and writers' workshops.

Our talented editor, Susan Bryant, did a wonderful job helping us to perfect this book. Her advice, friendship, and encouragement kept us going forward, and making it to the finished line.

The National Association of Memoir Writers, Linda Joy Myers, and Brooke Warner have been invaluable in helping us to grow as writers, and to seek and find a publisher. We also want to acknowledge the P2P course from DIY MFA, and Gabriela and her staff for helping us to understand all that we need to promote this book, and the books to come.

We are very grateful to Betty and Wally Turnbull and the staff of Light Messages and Torch Flame Publishing, for guiding us to make this manuscript into a great book. Their expertise and experience have been a big help to us. Working with them on this project has been very rewarding.

About the Authors

Crystal and Ron Meinstein are retired empty nesters living in a small village near Coshocton, Ohio with their 3-year-old, very smart, affectionate cat, Ella. Ron's career includes three degrees: Chemistry B.S., M. B.A. and RN and many occupations. He has worked as a chemist, lab manager, supervisor, health and safety director and in his 50's and 60's as an RN. They have lived in Illinois, Michigan, Indiana, and Ohio.

Crystal graduated from Bradley University, Magna Cum Laude as an English major. She has been an editor, secretary, researcher, crafts teacher, public speaker, but mainly a stay at home mom, raising their three daughters:

Elizabeth, Michelle, and Lisa. As a writer of poetry, essays, short stories and articles, she has been published in literary magazines, a national quilting magazine, and the 2017 and 2020 Coshocton Literary Review magazine editions. Her textile artwork has been shown in many quilt shows and art venues.

Their blog is full of family stories, humor, cat tales, their travel adventures and includes many beautiful photographs.

Connect with Ron and Crystal at:
marriagememoir.com

www.ingramcontent.com/pod-product-compliance
Lightning Source LLC
LaVergne TN
LVHW091132080826
845145LV00008B/2123

* 9 7 8 1 6 1 1 5 3 3 8 7 3 *